Bon

Peter St

Peter Straughan was writer-in-residence at Live Theatre in Newcastle in 1999/2000 where he wrote *Bones*. His play *Cold*, a black comedy about a string quartet of psychopathic young men toured during 2001 to great acclaim. His feature films *Five Psychopaths* and *The Edward Stark Trilogy* are under commission from Contagious Films. His half-hour television film *Waiters* was broadcast in 2001 starring Lee Hall and Robson Green. He won the Alfred Bradley radio award for the adaptation of his own stage play *The Ghost of Frederico Garcia Lorca Which Can Also Be Used As A Table*. The radio version was broadcast on BBC Radio 3 in 2001. Other plays include *Fetish* (Live Theatre, Newcastle, 2000), *Rat* (Pink Pony Theatre, New York, 1996), and *A Rhyme for Orange* (winner of the 1997 North East People's Play Award). He has also won several awards for short prose fiction.

Methuen Drama

Published by Methuen 2002

1 3 5 7 9 10 8 6 4 2

First published in the Great Britain in 2002
by Methuen Publishing Limited
215 Vauxhall Bridge Road,
London SW1V 1EJ

Methuen Publishing Limited Reg. No. 3543167

A CIP catalogue record is available from the British Library

ISBN 0 413 772047

Typeset by SX Composing DTP, Rayleigh, Essex
Printed and bound in Great Britain by
Cox & Wyman Ltd, Reading, Berkshire

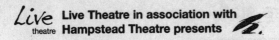

Live theatre **Live Theatre in association with Hampstead Theatre presents**

BONES

Written by Peter Straughan

Cast in order of appearance

Ruben Jonathan Slinger
Reg David Cardy
Moon Michael Hodgson
Beck Trevor Fox
Benny Deka Walmsley

Director Max Roberts
Production Design Perry John Hudson
Original music Olly Fox

**Performed at Live Theatre
from 26 February - 15 March 2002**

**Performed at Hampstead Theatre
from 20 March - 13 April 2002**

Bones was first produced at Live Theatre
in May 1999 as part of Peter Straughan's term
as Writer in Residence.

live theatre staff

Jim Beirne Executive Director
Max Roberts Artistic Director
Wendy Barnfather Finance & Admin Manager
Chris Durant Technical Manager
Jeremy Herrin Associate Director, New Writing
Paul James Associate Director, Live Lines
Sarah McPhail Marketing & Sales Manager
Carole Wears House Manager
Degna Bailey Administrator
Kath Boodhai Deputy House Manager
Sarah Clarke Press & Marketing Officer
Laura Lindow Resident Drama Worker, Live Lines
Catherine Moody Box Office Supervisor
Harriet Morgan Administrator, Live Lines
Tearlach Duncanson Outreach Drama Worker, Live Lines

live theatre board

Chris Bailey Head of School of Humanities,
University of Northumbria (Chair)
Gez Casey Writer and Actor
Michael Chaplin Writer/Television Producer
Tim Flood General Manager, Whitley Bay Playhouse
Cathy Franklin Head of Drama, Ryton Comprehensive School
Ken Hunt Partner, Hunt Kidd Solicitors (Vice Chair)
Sandra Jobling Television Producer, Coastal Productions
Ken Linge Director of Finance, Northern Electric
Carol Meredith Freelance Consultant
Sheila Spencer Newcastle City Councillor
Graeme Thompson Director of Broadcasting, Tyne Tees TV
David Whittaker Actor

Live theatre small theatre **big ideas**

Live Theatre explores ideas in new writing. We believe in relationships with writers and in the development of new writing. We are passionate about transforming these ideas into performance of the highest quality for stage and also for radio, film and television.

Live Theatre has its roots in the identity of the North of England creating and presenting work that is challenging, popular and of relevance to all.

Our venue is accessible and friendly, providing an arts programme that is unique to Newcastle and the North East. We engage all sectors of the community as participants and audiences. Live Theatre seeks to deliver this programme through a series of regional, national and international partnerships.

history

Live Theatre Company was formed in 1973. It has developed a strong national reputation for developing and nurturing new writing in the north of England. Over the last 28 years the company has forged relationships with a number of writers including CP Taylor, Sid Chaplin, Tom Hadaway, Leonard Barras, Alan Plater, and more recently Peter Flannery, Michael Chaplin, Karin Young, Lee Hall, Peter Straughan, Julia Darling and Sean O'Brien. Many well known actors have an association with Live Theatre including Tim Healey, who was one of the company's founder members, Denise Welch and Robson Green who gives substantial financial support to Live Lines - Live Theatre's training and outreach department.

The company has been based in premises on Newcastle's quayside since 1982. Over the last 20 years, the company's premises have grown to accommodate a theatre space, rehearsal room, company offices, café-bar and restaurant.

radio, television and film

**As well as presenting work for the stage, Live Theatre has
forged partnerships with broadcast media and film. In the
last year, Live was involved in the following projects;**

May 2001 BBC Radio 3 recorded *Laughter When We're Dead*, a play
written by Sean O'Brien and commissioned and produced by
Live Theatre in 2000.

July 2001 Live Theatre's Artistic Director, Max Roberts, made his
TV directorial debut with a short TV drama by Peter Straughan, called
Waiters, which was broadcast to the Tyne Tees, Yorkshire and
Granada television regions.

Summer 2001 Live acted as Production Associates on a new
film project with Assassin Films. *The One & Only*, written by
Peter Flannery was given script development support by Live in 2000.

October 2001 BBC announced its investment in Live Theatre as part
of *Northern Exposure*, to plan a two year programme of support and
events for writers in the region. This includes a development project
to create new drama product for BBC television.

December 2001 BBC Radio 4 broadcast three new plays about
philosophers, live from the theatre. The plays were written by
Sean O'Brien and Julia Darling (Live's current Writers In Residence)
and Peter Straughan.

new writing

Live Theatre is currently involved in partnerships for creative projects
with *Northern Stage, Hampstead Theatre*, the *Elements Drama
Initiative County Durham, The Royal Shakespeare Company* and the
BBC. A production of Lee Hall's *Cooking With Elvis*, directed by
Max Roberts, has just completed a 15-week number 1 national tour
and Alan Plater's *Tales from the Backyard* has just completed a sell
out run at Live.

The company has recently gained significant new investment from its
regular stakeholders to invest in its creative programme. The principle
focus of these new resources is into the development of writers and
new writing. This will enable Live Theatre to stage more productions,
to make more commissions, and to provide strategies and services
for developing writing talent regionally and nationally.

education & participation

In 1998, the company set up an education, training and outreach department, Live Lines. This department, co-ordinates the activities of the Live Youth Theatre which has over 200 current members, Live Wires, the over 50s writing and performance group and Live writers, a writing group for young people. This department delivers one of the largest arts participation programmes in Newcastle, with over 5000 individual training sessions annually. The department also works with a large number of partners in the community.

Live Lines is supported by Coastal Productions, Granada Media and the Northern Rock Foundation.

Live Theatre is supported by

For more information about Live Theatre or to join our mailing list call 0191 232 1232 or email info@live.org.uk

Live Theatre
27 Broad Chare
Quayside,
Newcastle upon Tyne
NE1 3DQ

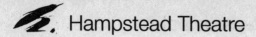 Hampstead Theatre

**At Hampstead Theatre new play writing is our passion.
For forty years we have been introducing new writers to the
world, whilst providing first class, affordable and accessible
entertainment to audiences of all ages.**

We read up to 1,800 scripts a year, encouraging, supporting and
developing dozens of new writers in the process. The best of these
we produce to the highest of standards, with the help of the best
actors, directors and designers. A play seen at Hampstead Theatre
is often only the beginning of the story. In just the last decade we
have: presented 101 plays, produced 71 premières, toured 13
productions and transferred 15 plays to the West End and
Broadway. We also collaborate with other theatres throughout the
country and are delighted to be working with Live Theatre for the
first time.

Some of our plays that have had a further life include:

Burn This by Lanford Wilson with John Malkovich

Someone Who'll Watch Over Me by Frank McGuinness

Dead Funny by Terry Johnson with Zoe Wanamaker

The Memory of Water by Shelagh Stephenson

Little Malcolm and His Struggle Against the Eunuchs
by David Halliwell with Ewan McGregor

Peggy For You by Alan Plater

Feelgood by Alistair Beaton

Since 1962 our home has been a now dilapidated portacabin
building in Swiss Cottage, North London. But now, having raised
£13 million, (including £9.85 million Lottery funds from the Arts
Council of England) we are in the process of building a new theatre.
Our new home will enable us to continue our crucial work in
developing writing talent and in working with the local community
through our education programme. The new building is on schedule
to be finished in autumn 2002 and will open in 2003.

If you would like details of our new building plans, details of how to
submit a play, or of our forthcoming productions - just visit our
website.

Hampstead Theatre 98 Avenue Road, London, NW3 3EX
Box Office - 020 7722 9301 www.hampstead-theatre.co.uk

peter straughan writer

Peter has worked with Live for a number of years and was the company's Writer in Residence in 1999.

Theatre credits include; *Cold* (The Ashton Group) *The Ghost of Federico Garcia Lorca Which Can Also Be Used As A Table* (Northern Stage), *Fetish - ne1* (Live Theatre), *Rat* (Pink Pony Theatre, New York) and *A Rhyme For Orange* (winner of the 1997 North East People's Play Award). He is currently under commission to Hampstead Theatre and to Live Theatre and Northern Stage who are co-producing a new play, *Noir*, in May 2002.

Peter's TV drama *Waiters* for Peter Mitchell Ltd/Tyne Tees Television/Northern Production fund was broadcast in July 2001.

Radio 4 have also produced his play *When We Were Queens* and his adaptation of Andrew Motion's *Wainewright The Poisoner* and *Centurions* (co-written with Bridget O'Connor)

Peter has completed writing his first feature film, *Five Psychopaths*, for Contagious Films, who have also commissioned a second film, *The Edward Stark Trilogy*.

In radio, Peter won the Alfred Bradley Award for his adaptation of his own stage play, *The Ghost of Federico Garcia Lorca*.

max roberts director

Max is the Artistic Director of Live Theatre, Newcastle upon Tyne. Favourite productions include; *The Long Line, Long Shadows* and *Seafarers* (Tom Hadaway), *Close The Coalhouse Door, Going Home, Shooting the Legend* and *Tales from the Backyard* (Alan Plater), *In Blackberry Time* (Alan Plater and Michael Chaplin from the stories of Sid Chaplin), *Twelve Tales of Tyneside* (Peter Flannery and others), *Northern Glory* (Phil Woods), *Laughter When We're Dead* (Sean O'Brien), *Only Joking* (Steve Chambers), *Buffalo Girls and Eggs and Basket Cases* (Karin Young) and *Cooking With Elvis* (Olivier Award Nominee - Best Comedy), *ne1* and *Wittgenstein on Tyne* (Lee Hall). Max is about to direct a new play by Peter Straughan entitled *Noir*, in a co-production with Northern Stage at Newcastle Playhouse.

cast

David Cardy Reg

Recent theatre includes; Sergeant Match in *What The Butler Saw* (National Tour), Arthur Hollis in *Why Me?* (National Tour), Agamemnon in *Troilus and Cressida* (Old Vic), *Pera Palas* (RNT Studio), Petruchio in *The Taming of the Shrew*, Sganarelle in *Don Juan* (English Touring Theatre), Pistol in *Chimes at Midnight* (Chichester Festival Theatre), Martin in *Nabokov's Gloves* (Hampstead Theatre), Budge in *The Shallow End* (Royal Court), Caliban in *The Tempest*, Antipholus of Syracuse in *The Comedy of Errors* (Regent's Park Open Air Theatre) and Sam Weller in *Pickwick* (Chichester Festival Theatre/tour/Sadler's Wells).

TV credits include: Mickey Freeman in *No Sweat*, Chris Theodopolopodous in *Birds of a Feather*, *Campaign*, *Vote for Them*, *The Chief I & II*, *Hard Cases*, *Nightingales*, *Stay Lucky*, *The Bill*, *London's Burning*, *Fool's Gold*, *The New Statesman*, *Safe*, *Eastenders*, *Absolutely Fabulous*, *Trial by Jury*, *Silent Witness*.

Film credits include: *Winds of War*, *The Keep*, *Xtro*, *Little Dorrit*, *Prick Up Your Ears*, *Three Steps To Heaven*, *Monk Dawson*.

Trevor Fox Beck

Trevor has had leading roles in many Live Theatre productions, including *Seafarers*, *Close the Coalhouse Door*, *Two*, *Oh What A Lovely War*, *Twelve Tales of Tyneside* , *ne1* and *Cooking With Elvis* at Live, in the West End and Number 1 tour.

Film credits include *Billy Elliot*, *Purely Belter* and *Gabriel & Me*.

TV credits include *Spender*, *Crocodile Shoes*, *Heartbeat*, *Our Friends in the North*, *The Student Prince*, *Peak Practice*, *Byker Grove* and *Touching Evil III*.

Radio credits include; *Blood Sugar*, *Think Tank*, *Skellig*, and *The Legend of Los Trombastardos* for BBC Radio 4 and Gristle for BBC Radio 3.

Michael Hodgson Moon

Michael's work for Live Theatre includes *My Last Barmaid - ne1* (Live Theatre and Newcastle Theatre Royal), *Fetish - ne1, Laughter When We're Dead* and the 1999 production of *Bones*. Other theatre work includes *Studs* (Hull Truck Theatre), *King Lear* (Young Vic/Tokyo Globe, Japan), *The Tower* (Almeida Theatre), *Wind in the Willows* and *The Devil's Disciple* (National Theatre), *Jane Eyre* (West End) and *The Guise* (Edinburgh, Hong Kong, New York - Winner of Fringe First Award 1990).

Television credits include: *Dalziel & Pascoe, Without Motive II, The Bill* (Guest Lead), *Touching Evil* and *The Tide of Life.*

Film credits include: *The One & Only, Purely Belter, The Lowdown, Wonderland* and *First Knight.*

Radio credits include: *Laughter When We're Dead* (BBC Radio 3) and *Barbarians* (BBC Radio 4)

Jonathan Slinger Ruben

Theatre credits include; *Richard II, Machine Wreckers* and *Widowers Houses* (Royal National Theatre), *The Winter's Tale* and *The Maid's Tragedy* (Shakespeare's Globe Theatre) and *As You Like It* (Royal Exchange).

Film credits include; *Spring Awakening, The Last September* and *A Knight's Tale.*

TV credits include: *Cold Feet, Out of Hours, Forgive and Forget* and *Stick With Me Kid.*

Radio credits include; *The Oresteia* and *High Wind in Jamaica* (BBC Radio 4)

Deka Walmsley Benny

Deka's work for Live Theatre includes: *ne1, Laughter When We're Dead, Some Voices, Long Shadows,* and *Tales from the Backyard.* Other theatre credits include; *Animal Farm* (Northern Stage), *Mapping The Edge* (WilsonWilson/Sheffield Crucible), 'Sammy' in *Blood Brothers* (West End) and *Cooking With Elvis* (West End).

TV credits include: *Rebus, Ticket To Ride, Our Friends in the North, Eastenders* and *Badger.*

Film credits include: *Dream On* and *Like Father.*

Deka has worked extensively for BBC Radio 3 & 4. Credits include: *Laughter When We're Dead, The Taming of the Shrew, A Midsummer Night's Dream* and *Frozen Images.*

Perry John Hudson Production Design

Perry trained at the Central School of Speech and Drama before working in the West End at *Her Majesty's Theatre*. He has worked extensively in the North East as a freelance designer. He has been Live Theatre's Associate Designer for the last 15 years. His work with Live Theatre includes *In Blackberry Time*, *Kiddars Luck*, *Hair in the Gate*, *Come Snow Come Blow*, *Buffalo Girls*, *Seafarers*, *Your Home in the West*, *Beautiful Game*, *For The Crack*, *Twelve Tales of Tyneside*, *Laughter When We're Dead*, *ne1*, *When We Were Queens* and *Tales from the Backyard*.

Pam Allan Company Stage Manager

Pam trained at the London Academy of Music and Dramatic Art and spent three years working in repertory theatre all over the country. She has toured Europe with *Michael Clarke Company* and *Yolande Snaith Theatre Dance*. Productions for Live Theatre include; *Shooting The Legend*, *Beautiful Game*, *Cabaret*, *Two*, *Oh What A Lovely War*, *All Credit to the Lads*, *Cooking With Elvis* and *ne1*. Other work includes Company Stage Manager for *The Royal Opera House* on *Mary Seacole* and Company Manager on *Rock n Roll Heaven* (national tour).

Gavin Frost Stage Manager

Gavin trained in Theatre & Media Production in Newcastle. He has worked as Stage Manager on various productions throughout the North East and further afield. Projects for Live Theatre include *For The Crack*, *Cooking With Elvis*, *Laughter When We're Dead*, *ne1*, *Tales from the Backyard* and various Live Lines productions. He has recently finished a national tour with children's theatre company, Monster *Productions*.

Olly Fox Music Composer

Olly works in theatre, radio and television as a composer. Some credits include: *The Good Woman of Setzuan* (Royal National Theatre), *Mr Kolpert* (The Royal Court), *The Way of the World* (Royal Exchange) and *Lifegame* (Improbable Theatre). Olly wrote the original score for the first production of *Bones* at Live Theatre in 1999. He has collaborated with Peter Straughan on several other productions including *Wainewright the Poisoner* and *The Ghost of Federico Garcia Lorca*, both for BBC Radio 4.

Lou Duffy Wardrobe

Lou is a costume designer who works on theatre and dance productions in the North East. She also works on various private commissions, clothing and accessory ranges. Lou worked on costumes for Live Theatre's *Tales from the Backyard.*

Terry King Fight Director

Terry has worked extensively in theatre and television, in particular with the Royal Shakespeare Company, the Royal National Theatre and The Royal Court. He has worked with some of the country's leading theatre directors including Sam Mendes, David Hare, Adrian Noble and Max Stafford Clark.

Theatre credits include; *Troilus and Cressida, Richard III, Romeo & Juliet, Macbeth* and *Othello* (RSC), *Fool for Love, The Murderers, King Lear, The Birthday Party, Waiting for Godot* and *The Riot* (Royal National Theatre), *The Recruiting Officer, The Queen and I, Search and Destroy* and *Berlin* (The Royal Court).

Television credits include; *Casualty, Eastenders, The Mayor of Casterbridge, Lucky Jim* and *A Kind of Innocence.*

Debbie Hunt Deputy Stage Manager

Debbie has worked as a DSM for the Palace Theatre, Westcliff for many productions including; *Fings Ain't Wot They Used T'be, Treasure Island* and *Macbeth* as well as productions in the 2001 Agatha Christie Festival including *Go Back For Murder, Appointment With Death, Yellow Iris* and *Personal Call.*

Other work includes *Ghostdancing* by Tamasha Theatre Company (London, national tour, Copenhagen) and *The Woman in Black* (PW Productions in association with Green and Lenagan Ltd).

Bones

For Bebe

Bones premiered at the Live Theatre, Newcastle on 4 May, 1999. The cast was as follows:

Reg	Colin Maclachlan
Ruben	Daymond Britton
Beck	Trevor Fox
Moon	Michael Hodgson
Benny	Derek Walmsley

Directed by Max Roberts
Designed by Perry Hudson

Act One

Prologue

As the house lights dim, we hear music. **Ruben** *appears. He stares at the audience.*

Ruben *God* . . . tells Abraham to, to *kill* his, his *only* son Isaac and (do you know this?) and, to, to prove his *faith.* (*Beat.*) So Abraham takes him up on the mountain, takes Isaac up, and he's just going to do it . . . to kill him . . . and an Angel comes down and says, say 'Abraham, you don't have to do it. You don't have . . . kill this *ram*, instead.' Because, because he'd proved himself . . . because he *would* have done it. He *would* have . . . (*Pause.*) And I thought about that, because, because I think it means, I think it means with, with *faith*, you can *change* yourself, make yourself do things that . . . *prove* yourself. You can become. (*Beat.*) You can become.

Scene One

We are in the lobby and bar of 'The Roma' – a porn cinema in sixties Gateshead. A young man – **Ruben** *is behind the desk. In front of him is* **Reg** *– talking on the phone.* **Reg** *is drunk. He has a small suitcase with him.*

Reg (*on phone*) Who am I? No . . . No . . . Who the fuck are you? Who? Put Harry on! No. Put Harry on, now! You're a fuckin liar. Put him on. Because I know your fucking address and if you don't put Harry on I'll come round and cut your fuckin eyes out! What? Hang on.

He takes out a piece of paper and reads it.

47714. Oh. OK.

He hangs up.

Wrong number.

Ruben   Right.

Reg   Anyway. Tarts.

Ruben   I'm sorry?

Reg *dials again.*

Reg   Tarts.

Ruben   Tarts?

Reg   Tarts. Whores. Berkely.

Ruben   This is a cinema.

Reg   Hang on . . . Put Harry on. What? Harry Morgan. Morgan M, O . . . How many Harrys live there? Well, that'll be him then, won't it, you stupid prick. Fuck me – what a . . . (*To* **Ruben**.) How much?

Ruben   How much?

Reg   For something to fuck. (*To phone.*) Harry? You know who this is. Yes, you do. Yes, you do. This is the man you were supposed to meet this afternoon. Yes, you were. No. No – *this* week. Because – because *I've* got it fuckin written down, that's how. I am looking at my diary and it says Boxing Day, one o'clock, meet a cunt. (*Beat*) Yeah? Well, I have spent my Christmas travelling to this shit-hole of the world. Don't . . . do not try and turn this on to me. I know this is Christmas – time of goodwill, time to be with family, time to toast your yuletide logs and give goodwill to all and I – I have spent my Christmas on a fucking train with five pissed Jocks to come to this – the shithole of the world. (*To* **Ruben**.) Where?

Ruben   Dunston.

Reg   Dunston . . . Where? Deckam? Where the fuck is that? You did not. (*Beat.*) Harry? Harry? Stop snivelling Harry. It's too late, son. I'm just ringing to tell you . . . You Are Fucked.

He hangs up. He looks at his watch.

Ruben   Sir, about . . .

Reg   Crying like a baby. Get them by the balls. I give him ten seconds before he rings back.

Pause. They stare at the phone.

Five . . . four . . . three . . . two . . . one.

Pause. They stare at the phone.

Ruben   Does he know where you are?

Reg   What?

Ruben   Um . . .He can't ring you back. He doesn't know where you are.

Reg   Cunt.

He goes to dial again then hangs up.

Who are you?

Ruben   I'm sorry?

Reg   You. Who are you?

Ruben   My name?

Reg   Not your. . . You. Who are you? What do you do?

Ruben   I'm the manager. Well, assistant manager. . .My brother . . .

Reg   You are a server. You provide services. I want cunt. Serve me cunt. (*Pause.*) What's that? What's that staring thing? Is that supposed to disturb me?

Ruben   Um . . . I think . . .

Reg   Is that supposed to make me feel ashamed? Is it? (*Pause.*) *Don't* stare at me.

Ruben   I'm just . . . er . . .

Pause.

Reg   Forget it. Forget the cunt. The moment's gone. You
have ruined the moment. Get me a drink. Serve me a drink.

Ruben   You have to be a . . . member . . . it's like a club
. . . like . . .

Pause.

What would you like?

Reg   Ginger Snatch.

Ruben   A . . . Right . . .

Pause.

Reg   What?

Ruben   What?

Reg   Where's my drink?

Ruben   I'm just . . . Ginger Snatch?

Reg   Yes.

Ruben   So that's . . .ginger and . . .

Reg   What can you do, son? What is your area of *expertise*?

Ruben   I'm not really . . .

Reg   Whiskey. Ginger. Champagne. Ice.

Ruben   Right . . . right . . .

He searches through the shelves behind him for the bottles.

Ruben   Uh . . . We don't . . . we don't have any
champagne . . .

Reg   What have you got?

Ruben   Fizzy?

Reg   Yes, son. Fizzy.

Ruben   Um . . . Babycham?

Beat.

Reg   Whisky. Ginger. Ice. Babycham.

Ruben   Right. Could you just sign the book, sir? Just . . . so you're a member.

Reg   I don't wanna be a member.

Ruben   It's just for the drink, sir. Just so I don't get into trouble, like.

Reg   Well, we wouldn't want you to get into trouble, would we? Give it here.

Ruben *pours the drink.* **Reg** *signs the book.* **Ruben** *gives him the drink.*

Reg   Bottoms up.

Ruben   Yeah, merry Christmas, Mr . . .

He reads the name in the book. **Reg** *downs the drink in one.*

. . . Jesus.

Reg (*thoughtfully*)   Tastes like kids' knickers.

Pause.

Ruben   You're . . . I didn't know. Jesus.

Reg *puts some money on the counter and turns to leave.*

Ruben   What? You're going? Don't you want to see a film?

Reg   No, I don't want to see a film. I want some cunt.

Ruben   But . . . But . . . Hang on . . .

Reg *is leaving.*

Ruben   I know someone.

Reg   What?

Ruben   A woman . . . I can get you a woman . . . for you, I mean. It would be . . . it would be . . .

Pause. **Reg** *comes back.*

Reg   Name?

Ruben   It's – um – Dolores.

Reg   Your name.

Ruben   Oh. My name. It's . . . it's, it's Frankie. Frankie.
DeSimone.

Reg   What's that? That wop?

Ruben   Yes. Yes, it is.

Reg   You a pimp, Frankie?

Ruben   No! No . . . but I mean, for you . . . No. Never.

Reg   How old is Dolores?

Ruben   Sixteen.

Reg   Sixteen? She look sixteen?

Ruben   Yes, she does. She does. She . . . um . . . why
don't you have a drink, on the house I mean, and we'll get
Dolores over and . . .

Reg   I have seen terrible sixteen-year-olds in my time. I
have seen some sixteen-year-old hounds in my time.

Ruben   I don't think you will be disappointed.

Reg   I hope not, Frankie. I have had a very bad
Christmas.

Reg *lifts up his suitcase and opens it. he shows the contents to*
Ruben. *Long pause.*

Reg   You know what they are?

Pause.

Ruben   I think so.

Reg   Yeah. (*Pause.*) Yeah.

Music.

Scene Two

The projection room. two young men are watching an old reel of
White Heat. *One,* **Moon**, *wears a gorilla suit. He is holding the*
head. The other, **Beck**, *is wearing a twenties style dress.*

Beck   Bollocks.

Moon   I'm just . . .

Beck   Bollocks.

Moon   Will you . . . do you mind if I talk?

Beck   I have heard some bollocks in my time . . .

Moon   I am just saying . . .

Beck   But *your* bollocks.

Moon   All right. How come then, in *Key Largo*, right, in *Key*
Largo, Bogart's on the boat with all the gangsters and that,
he's only get got like a little pistol and he shoots them all,
right? Beats them all up and that? They didn't cast Cagney
for it, did they? Because . . .

Beck   Bollocks.

Moon   Because they knew that nobody would believe that
Cagney could take on all them gangsters on account of him
being about four-foot tall and soft as shite . . .

Beck   If you remember, Moon, those gangsters happened
to be lead by Edward G. Robinson.

Moon   So?

Beck   So? I could chin Edward G. Robinson, man. My
fucking mother could chin Edward G. Robinson. Cagney
wouldn't waste his fucking time on Edward G. Robinson.
They probably offered the part to Cagney and he probably
said, 'You're joking, aren't you? Give it to that puff, Bogart.'

Moon   Just watch your film, will you? Just watch your
film.

Pause. They stare at the film. **Beck** *checks his watch.*

Moon   You think he's alright?

Beck   Fuck knows. (*Beat.*) Stupid get. (*Beat.*) I wouldn't've let it get this far. Four weeks fuckin' money. (*Beat.*) Well, I'll tell you something. They come for me and I'm off. I'm not getting a kicking for him. Fucking Benny. You know what I mean?

Moon   I like him.

Beck   *I* like him. What the fuck's that got to do with it? *I* like him. I'm saying though he's a useless cunt. They'll take this place over, you know. Then we're out of a job.

Moon   Eh? What for?

Beck   What do you think? Landers' not gonna keep us on, is he?

Moon   I don't see why not. This is nowt to do with us. We're just doing our jobs. And I can't afford to lose my job. I'm gonna be a father.

Beck   You what? With who?

Moon   Debbie! Who do you think?

Beck   What are you talking about? You told me you weren't even shagging her.

Moon   I told you, that's a secret! We're waiting, aren't we? But I mean, we're talking about it. We've been looking at prams and that.

Beck   This is what I'm saying. He's gonna fuck it up for all of us. Pissing around with Landers. Stupid get. (*Pause.*) Should never have got involved. I know Landers. Should have let me deal with it.

Moon   Right.

Beck   I know stuff. I could've dealt with him. I wouldn't have let it go this far. Stupid get.

Moon   I like him.

Beck   Hey, man – I like him. But – this is what I'm saying – He's a four-by-two – you can't get away from that. He's probably hiding the money. Serve him right if they do him in. Fucking Jews.

Moon   Tony Curtis is a Jew.

Beck   Fuck off.

Moon   He is.

Beck   Oh, Fuck Off. You don't get Italian Jews.

Moon   He's not Italian.

Beck   Excuse me? Tony Curtis isn't Italian? Curtis is a Jew name?

Moon   Curtis isn't his real name.

Beck   Oh, Fuck Off.

Moon   I read it.

Beck   He doesn't even *look* like a Jew. (*Beat.*)

Benny, *an older man, enters behind them. He is holding a handkerchief to a bleeding nose and carries an empty bottle of whisky. He searches some reels for something.*

Beck   Benny? How'd it go?

Benny   Have you seen a . . . there was a . . . there was a half bottle up here.

Moon   What's that Benny?

Benny   Whiskey. There was a half bottle up here. Have you moved it?

Moon   There's some in the bar.

Benny   There isn't. It's finished. *Fucking* . . . have you moved it?

He turns round and notices their costumes.

Benny (*to* **Beck**) What . . . what are you wearing?

Beck   Dress. (*Pause.*) It's comedy.

Benny   You look like a wanker.

Beck   You said to come in fancy dress!

Benny   On the theme of movies! What fucking movie are you?

Beck   *Some Like It Fucking Hot*! (*Beat.*) And what about the clip of this cunt? What the fuck is he supposed to be?

Moon   King Kong. It's horror. How'd it go?

Benny   How's it look like it fucking went? They gave me one week and a kick in the face.

Beck   One week? For all of it? How the fuck are you going to get the money?

Benny   I don't know . . . maybe . . . What the fuck are you? Private Eye? And while we're on twenty questions, what are you doing watching Jimmy Cagney movies? We're supposed to be a porn cinema. And why aren't you ushering?

Moon   Who am I going to usher? There's no one in.

Benny   I'm trying to run a business here, you know? There's no one on the door? What do I pay you two for?

Beck   *What?* You *don't* fucking pay us. I haven't had any fucking wages for two weeks! And Moon here's gonna be a father soon!

Benny   Since when? You told me he wasn't even shagging her.

Moon   Fuck's sake, Beck! I said it was a secret!

Beck   All I'm saying, Benny, is that we have obligations here.

Benny   I'm bleeding here, Beck! I've put seven years into this dump and I'm standing here bleeding! I don't need to be getting it in the ear off you two, alright? I need some . . . I need some fuckin' help, here!

(*Pause.*) **Moon** *picks up a kettle.*

Moon   I'll make us a cuppa, eh?

Benny *sits down. He seems exhausted.*

Benny   Tell Ruben I need to see him.

Moon *exits.*

Beck, go and get me some whiskey. Me nose is fucking killing me.

Beck   Listen Benny . . . do you want me to have a word with Landers? I mean, no offence – but these are my people, you know what I mean?

Benny   Beck . . .

Beck   I mean, I understand how they work and that. When I was doing my time, I was in with Billy Turnbull, and his brother works for Landers and that and . . .

Benny   Hey, Al Capone! You did three months for shoplifting, so let's not get too carried away here.

Beck   What I'm saying is . . .

Benny   Just do what I ask, will you. For once.Get me the whiskey.

Beck *hesitates then leaves. From the sound track of* White Heat *we hear Cagney:* 'Stuffy, huh? I'll give it some air!'

We hear the shots Cagney is firing in the film. **Benny** *stares bleakly at the screen.*

Scene Three

At the front desk. **Ruben**, *stands staring straight ahead. He is wearing* **Reg**'s *coat. Music ends.* **Moon** *appears.*

Moon   Benny's wants to see you, Ruben (**Ruben** *stares at him vaguely.*) Ruben. Who've you come as?

Ruben   (*Beat.*) . . . What?

Moon   The coat? Who've you come as?

Ruben   I . . . um . . I forgot.

Moon   Right. I'm King Kong. It's horror. Beck's come as a wanker.

He heads towards the back room.

Ruben   Where – Where are you going?

Moon   Getting some water. Benny wants a cuppa.

Ruben   You can't.

Pause.

Moon   I can't?

Ruben   No. (*Pause.*)

Moon   I'm just getting some water.

Ruben   No. You can't.

Moon   Why can't I get some water?

Ruben   Because . . . because I think you should go home, Moon.

Moon   You what?

Ruben   I think you should go home.

Moon   (*Beat.*) Why?

Ruben   (*Beat.*) It's Christmas.

Moon   (*Beat.*) Are you pissed?

Ruben   No.

Moon   Well, what you going on about then? I'm making a cuppa.

Ruben   Wa . . . No, Moon!

Moon *has already gone into the backroom.*

Pause. **Ruben** *rests his head against the desk.*

Ruben (*softly*)   Fuck, fuck, fuck.

Moon *reappears. Pause.*

Moon   Ruben?

Ruben   I know. I know.

Pause.

Moon   I want to go home now.

Ruben   Moony . . .

Moon   No, really, I mean it . . . I . . . whatever it is . . . you said I could go home.

Ruben   I – uh . . . I don't think you can now, Moony.

Moon   You said you wanted me to go.

Ruben   Yeah. Well, now I don't think you can.

Moon   Rube?

Ruben   Yeah?

Moon   What's going on?

Ruben   It's . . um . .. it's some business.

Moon   Have you been getting your headaches again?

Ruben   Don't.

Moon   If you are (I'm just saying, right?), if you are, I want you to tell me, that's all . . . and . . . and . . . and . . . fucking hell, Abe, what the fuck is –

Ruben   I know. I know. (*Beat.*) Now just . . . just calm
down.

You want a fag? Just calm down. I need you to keep quiet
about this, all right? I can explain this.

Moon   Yeah? It better be a fucking good explanation, 'cos
Benny's gonna . . I mean, he's gonna . . .

Benny (*appearing*)   Benny's gonna what? (*Pause.*) Moon?

Ruben   (*Pause.*) Moon said you wanted to see me.

Benny   Why weren't you on the door?

Ruben   I was just . . .

Benny   Place's fuckin' wide open.

Benny   I'm sorry.

Pause.

Benny   Listen, Ruben, we've gotta . . . we've gotta . . .

*He notices **Moon** is still there.*

Moon? I thought you were making some tea?

Moon   Right, I'm just . . .

He moves towards the store room door. He stops.

Benny (*to **Benny***)   Listen, Ruben. I've been thinking and
. . . uh . . . I think it's time to call it a day.

Ruben   This is our place Benny. They're not getting it.

Benny   Ruben, Ruben . . .

Ruben   Seven years, Benny

Benny   It's just a place, Ruben.

Ruben   It's *our* place!

Benny   I *can't* get the money, Ruben! I've tried and . . . (*he
notices that **Moon** is still standing in front of the store room door*) . . .
and . . . Moon?

Moon   Yeah, Benny?

Benny   You turn the round metal bit and the big flat wooden bit opens up.

Moon   Yeah. Right, I'll just, uh, right.

He heads for the main entrance.

Benny   Where are you going?

Moon   I'm just going to use the tap in the bogs.

Benny   Why?

Moon   I think, I think, I think the water's better there.

Benny   Right.

Moon *goes to leave.*

Moon.

Moon   Yeah, Benny?

Benny   Lots of milk.

Moon   Right.

He goes to leave.

Benny   Moon?

Moon   Yeah?

Benny   Three sugars.

Moon   Three sugars. Right.

He goes to leave.

Benny   Moon?

Moon   Yeah, Benny?

Benny   What's in the backroom?

Moon   The backroom?

Benny   Yeah, the backroom. Why don't you want to go into the backroom?

Moon   I . . . there's nothing in there really, is there Ruben? Just some, you know, old stuff–tables, barrels . . .

Benny *walks over to the back room and goes in. Silence.*

Ruben   Listen, when he comes out, just let me do the talking.

Moon   Good. Fine. Good. This is nothing to do with me, anyway.

Ruben   You see?

Moon   What?

Ruben   You see? This is what I mean.

Moon   What?

Ruben   This is why we're fucking nobodies. This is exactly what's going to have to change!

Moon   Ruben . . . come on, calm down . . .

Ruben   We don't stick together. We never sticks together! Have I ever let you down?

Moon   I'm sorry, Ruben.

Ruben   I'm just saying, you know? United we stand, divided we fall.

Moon   Absolutely. I'm sorry.

Benny *comes back out. Silence. He stares at* **Moon**.

Moon (*pointing at* **Ruben**)   It was him.

Ruben   Jesus, Moon!

Moon   It was him, Benny – the fucking psycho.

Benny   Shut up.

Silence.

Some old reels, some tables, some mops, a large naked man tied to a chair. (*Beat.*) Anything you have to tell me, Ruben?

Ruben   Yes. I was . . . Well first of all . . . he was *already* pissed and he said he wanted a drink and so I . . . I saw the name – he even underlined the Reg – so we get chatting and he says he wants a woman, so I tell him to stay here and I'll get Dolores for him and . . .

Benny   Who?

Ruben   Dolores.

Benny   Who?

Ruben   I made her up.

Benny   Go on.

Ruben   So, he has a couple more drinks and then he goes and passes out and, and, I tie him to a chair in the back room and . . .that's it.

Benny   That's it? (*Pause.*) That's what? What the . . . He's fucking naked! He's tied to a chair!

Ruben   I just . . . I just didn't want him leaving. (*Pause.*) Reg. (Pause.) Now do you see?

Benny   Yeah. I've got it. Have you got it, Moon?

Moon   Um . . .

Benny   Reg. Anyone called Reg we nick their trolleys, lock 'em in the back room. We hate those Regniks.

Ruben   No – No – Benny, this isn't just any Reg . . .

Benny   Ruben, Ruben, I don't care if this is King Reg of Reggie Land, the point I'm trying to make is –

Ruben   It's Reggie Kray.

Benny   – is that – is that (*Pause. He laughs.*) Reggie Kray. (*He laughs.*) Reggie. Kray. (*He laughs. Beat.*) Have you been getting your headaches?

Ruben   No.

Moon   That's what I said, Benny! That's just what I said!

Benny   I'm just – shut up, Moon – I'm just asking you.

Moon   First thing I said!

Benny   Shut the fuck up! Now, Ruben. I'm asking you.
Are you ill again?

Ruben   Fuck sake, Benny! I'm not like that any more!

Benny   All right. All right. Listen.

Ruben   All right.

Benny   Reggie Kray, right?

Ruben   Right.

Benny   Reggie Kray, right? Big Gangster. Very Big.
Bigger then Mr Landers. Right?

Ruben   Don't.

Benny   And Reggie Kray (Big Gangster) lives in London
right? Which is a big city in the South where cockneys come
from and eels and shit, right?

Ruben   Benny . . .

Benny   Right. Now, imagine you're Reggie Kray in
London, right? And you're fancying a pint, right? (*He laughs.*)
You're fancying a pint and you're thinking (*he laughs*) (fuck
me), you're thinking – Where shall I go for a pint? – cor
blimey apples and fucking pears – Shall I go down the
fucking Cockney Arms – down me fucking local – Shall I go
there, right? Or, shall I – let's see – shall I get on the four
thirty to Newcastle and have a pint in Gateshead. Yeah,
yeah, I think I'll do that!

Moon *laughs.* **Benny** *stares at him.* **Moon** *stops laughing.*

Benny   No. You're not, are you? You're not really going
to do that. So you see, Benny, I think that bloke in there

probably isn't Reggie Kray. I think you're probably a
spastic.

Ruben   He *is* Reggie Kray . . .

Benny   I mean, I don't blame you entirely for this because
you know how mams have cravings when they're pregnant ?
For example, Mameh loved bananas when she was having
me and – the thing is Mam sniffed paint when she was
having you – so I'm not going to blame you entirely for this.
I'm going to blame Mameh for this. I'm going to blame
Mameh and Dulux for this. Fuck me. I don't believe this
day.

Ruben   It is Reggie Kray. . .

Benny   SHUT THE FUCK UP, YOU PUTZ! You seen
my face? We've got one week to get Landers his money.
One week. I'm a little worried all ready. And this – this I
could have done without.

Ruben   Benny . . .

Benny   Ruben – you're my brother. But if you say one
more fucking word to me – I swear to God I'll kill you
myself.

Ruben   OK, OK. Look, I can prove it to you. He had
something with him. He showed me. Let me go and get it.
OK? Just look at what he had with him and tell me he isn't
who he says he is.

Ruben *goes into the back room.*

Moon   Benny? Can I say something here?

Benny   What?

Moon   Now, you know I love Ruben – I do – I mean he's
like a brother to me – you know that – I'd do anything for
Ruben, I'd – hell and high water – and . . .

Benny   What do you want to say, Moon?

Moon   I think he's a nutter. Now, when I say that I mean
it in a – you know – like a medical way. I think he really
might be going funny again . . . I mean – this is fucking
kidnapping – and Reggie Kray, for fuck's sake. He's losing
it.

Beck *enters and comes up behind* **Benny**.

Beck   Benny?

Benny   (*Jumping*) JESUS! Beck! What the . . . Don't do
that! How many times am I telling you – don't come up
behind a man.

Beck   All right, all right! I'm just bringing you your
whisky. You'll never guess what I heard.

Moon   Never mind what you've heard. You'll never guess
what fucking Ruben's done!

Benny (*to* **Moon**)   Will you shut your gob?

Beck   About Landers.

Moon   Beck – I'm saying – You'll never fucking guess
what Ruben's done –

Benny   What about him?

Beck   Tony says he's fucking foaming. He's called a
meeting of all the boys.

Moon   Right, he's only gone and locked some poor fucker
in the back room, yeah? But this is the best bit –

Benny   What are you talking about?

Beck   There were some visitors yesterday.

Moon   Guess who he thought the bloke was –

Beck   Landers wants them scared off, permanently. He's
fucking livid. He says he'll go to war over this.

Moon   Go on, have a guess . . .

Benny (*quietly*.)   Who were the visitors?

Moon   Go on. You'll never guess!

Beck   The Krays.

Moon   He only thinks he's gone and kidnapped Reg – he thinks he's – he thinks . . .

Long silence. **Benny** *and* **Moon** *stare at the back room.*

Moon (*softly*)   We're dead.

Benny   Shut up, Moon.

Moon   We're dead. We are all fucking dead. We are all already fucking dead.

Benny   Shut up!

Beck   What's he ranting about?

Moon   We look like we're still alive but that's just a fucking optical whatsitsname because we are fucking dead as as as fucking dead things . . .

The back room door opens. **Ruben** *comes out carrying* **Reg**'s *suitcase. He crosses to the others and opens the case – showing them what is inside. Pause.*

Ruben   You know what they are?

The others nod slowly.

Yeah. (*Beat.*) Yeah.

Silence. the others stare at him. He stares back. Music.

Scene Four

Reception. **Benny** *throttles* **Ruben** *over a table.* **Moon** *tries to stop him.* **Beck** *is at the door to the back room trying to listen.*

Moon   Benny! Benny! This isn't helping anything.

Benny   It is! It's helping me!

Ruben (*choking*)   Benjamin! *Gevalt!*

Benny   Don't get Jewish on me! You're not a Jew. No Jew could be so fucking stupid!

Moon   He's going blue, Benny!

Benny *lets him go.*

Benny   Great fucking Christmas! Your eggs hard-boiled, pissing down with snow, you get kicked in the face, your brother kidnaps Reggie Kray.

Ruben   I didn't kidnap him, all right? He passed out and . . .

Beck   Reggie Kray. Fucking incredible. And no one was with him when he came in?

Ruben   No. I told you.

Beck   I don't believe this! He just wanders in and no one knows he's here.

Benny   What are you trying to do to me? You're a kidnapper, now? No. You're Ruben Stein. You work in a porn cinema. In Gateshead. You're a Jew for fuck's . . .

Ruben   If you would just (I'm Italian.) if you would . . .

Benny   Oh, will you stop it with the . . .

Ruben   I'm an Italian . . .

Benny   My father, God rest him, brought you up to be . . .

Ruben   That shit was not my father! My dad was Italian!

Benny   Oh, for . . . How the fuck do you know?

Ruben   Mameh told me!

Benny   How the fuck would she know who your dad was? Some fucking GI? Mam didn't ask for passports – you know? I mean, I loved her dearly, God *bentsch* her sacred name, but for a Jew, Mameh was some fucking slut.

Ruben   You think what you like, Benny, OK? But me –
I'm not who I was, OK? From now on, don't even call me
Ruben.

Benny   I wasn't going to call you Ruben. The name
'shithead' sprang to mind . . .

Ruben   I've changed my name. I want you to call me
Frankie.

Moon   You want us to call you Frankie Stein?

Beat.

Ruben   No, Moon. I want you to call me Frankie
DeSimone.

Moon   Who?

Ruben   I . . . I made it up, all right? But that's . . .that's
OK. You can give yourself a new name . . . like actors.
Because I know that Reggie Kray coming here, that's like a
sign. That's like a sign from my real father. That was like
him saying to me – Here, son, start again. This time, be
someone. Become Someone.

Benny   That's nice. I'm sure he's very pleased with your
new career as fucking psychopath. What are we . . .

Beck   Shhh!

Silence.

I think I heard something.

They join him at the door.

Benny   What did you hear?

Beck   I dunno. It was . . . I think it was like a – like a click.

Benny   A click?

Beck   A click- you know – a fucking click like a . . . like . . .

Moon   Like a gun.

Benny Don't say . . . Moon? Do you have to say that?

Moon Oh Jesus.

Beck I didn't say that.

Benny He didn't say that!

Moon He's got a fucking gun.

Ruben He hasn't got a gun. I searched him.

Moon Yeah? You look everywhere? You look

in his socks?

Ruben What?

Moon You didn't check his socks? Oh, fuck me. It's
Reggie fucking Kray – he has guns everywhere – up his
arse . . .

Benny What?

Moon They do. I read it. Keep a barrel up their arse,
magazine in the sock.

Benny Why the fuck would he have a gun in his arse?

Moon In case he . . . you know . . . in case he meets
fucking Ruben.

Beck Will you shut up. (*Pause.*) It's not a click – it's a – it's
a tick.

Moon Oh my God. Something's ticking. It's . . . he's got
a fucking bomb. Oh Sweet Jesus.

Benny Yeah, right, Moon. They do that – gangsters.
Keep bombs up their arse. It's the clock in back room, you
prick.

Beck Oh, yeah. It is. I can hear it now.

Moon Listen – Benny – Please let's, let's just go – Eh? He
doesn't know who we are. Let's just fucking untie him and
fuck off! We could, couldn't we?

Beck Yeah, we could do that, Moon. We could even put a note on him, saying, 'Sorry we took your kegs.' You fucking prick. He's not a packet of Woodbines! We haven't robbed fucking Woolies! We can't put him back and run off!

Moon Am I talking to you? I'm not fucking talking to you!

Benny Moon! Please! Be calm.

Moon I'm sorry, Benny. I'm sorry. I'm just shitting myself. I just, I just keep remembering what John said. You know? I mean his cousin's mate's sister was in a club in London where Reggie took someone's face off for talking to him. Took it off. Plop. On the floor. For talking to him! I mean, I don't think I can even work out what someone like that does to people who keep them in a cupboard . . .

Beck Benny? Will you shut him up?

Benny Why Ruben? *Why* would you *do* this?

Ruben For, for, for you! I did it for you!

Benny You did it for me?

Ruben For us! You said yourself, they're gonna take the place off us! All our lives Benny . . . I'm not . . . I'm not taking it anymore. We're gonna fight back!

Benny You're not a gangster, Ruben! You're a Jew!

Ruben Jews can fight back too! Like, like Masada!

Benny All the Jews *died* at the end of Masada you prick!

Beck Wait a minute. I heard something! He moved.

They rush to the door and listen.

Moon I don't . . .

Beck Shh! (*Pause.*) There! It's like – like a – moan . . .

Benny Breathing – I can hear breathing!

Moon   Oh my God! He must just be on the other side of the door.

Beat. They all move away from the door.

Benny   Ruben?

Ruben   Yeah?

Benny   He's tied, isn't he? You tied him, right?

Ruben   Yes!

Beat.

Benny   What knot?

Ruben   What?

Benny   I'm asking you! What knot? Sheep shank? Granny knot?

Ruben   I . . . What am I? Fucking Girl Guide? I tied him!

Moon   Oh shit.

Benny   What? What?

Moon   That click. He had a knife. He had a flickie up his arse.

Benny   Will you leave the arse thing? What is it with you and gangsters' arses?

Moon   I'm telling you. He's cut himself free. The last noise I'm gonna hear is my face going plop on the floor.

Beck   Ruben?

Ruben   What?

Beck   You locked the door right?

Beat.

Ruben   Yeah.

Beck   What's that mean? You paused. What does that mean?

Ruben   I – I – I locked the door.

Beck   Now he's stammering. What the fuck does that mean? Is the door locked?

Ruben   I think so.

Benny   Fuck me.

Ruben   Hey! Hey! Pardon me. I had a little bit on me mind there.

Benny   Yeah, right, Ruben. Only one thing – like a kind of rule. You're gonna lock up a Reggie Kray, you have to remember to turn the key. Fuck me.

Ruben   This is what I mean. This is why we're nobodies. We have no faith in ourselves. I Locked The Door, OK?

*He is naked and blindfolded with his hands tied. He walks forward trying to pull off his blindfold. The door opens and **Reg** walks out. Before he can manage this he comes into contact with a petrified **Beck**. He reaches out and runs his hands over **Beck** and up to the wig. Beat.*

Reg   Please. Tell me you're not Dolores.

Ruben   Um . . . Mr Kray? I can explain this. You passed out, you see, and . . .

Reg   You know who I am?

Ruben   I . . . Yes.

Reg   You know who I am?

Ruben   Yes. We do and . . .

Reg *grabs **Beck** by the throat.*

Reg   You know who I am? You know who I fucking am?

Benny *rushes forward to help.* **Reg** *head butts him and he falls.* **Ruben** *and* **Moon** *stand frozen as* **Reg** *throttles* **Beck**.

Reg   You know who I Fucking am?

Beck (*choking*)   Ruben! Moony! Jesus!

Moon *grabs a large papier-mache boy from beside the desk and smashes it over* **Reg**'s *head.* **Reg** *falls to the ground.* **Beck** *staggers, holding his throat.* **Benny** *lies on the ground holding his nose. Pause.* **Ruben** *kneels beside* **Reg** *and checks his breathing.*

Moon   Fucking hell, I've – With a plastic – Fucking hell . . . I've killed him. I've killed him with a fucking . . . with a placca spacca lad.

Ruben   You haven't. He's still breathing.

He begins to drag **Reg** *into the back room.*

Moon   Is he? Thank fuck. I thought I'd . . . (*Pause.*) I've hit Reg Kray. I've – hit – Reginald – Kray.

Beck (*with difficulty*)   I'll tell you this – he's fucking lucky Moon hit him there, 'cos I was just about to have him.

Benny   Jesus Christ! My fucking nose! He's broken my fucking nose. Twice in one fucking day!

Moon   And that was for charity. You're not supposed to open those. Fucking little spastic kids and that!

Benny   Moon! Moon! Fuck The Caliper Kid! I'm bleeding to death here!

Moon   I feel sick. I feel . . . I think I've shat myself.

Beck   Shut the fuck up, Moony man!

Pause. **Ruben** *gives* **Benny** *his handkerchief.*

Ruben   Here.

Benny *climbs to his feet.*

Moon   Benny? What are we going to do?

Benny   I don't . . . I don't know. I don't . . . we get the, we get the van.

Ruben *comes back out.*

Ruben   Benny . . .

Benny   Beck, go and get the van and you and Moon, you take him somewhere . . .

Moon   What? Me?

Ruben   Benny, I think we've crossed a line here . . .

Moon   I'm not . . . I'm not . . .

Benny   You take him somewhere and you dump him and . . .

Moon   I'm not taking him! Where am I gonna . . . ?

Ruben   Benny, we can't let him go.

Benny   SHUT UP! (*To* **Moon**.) We've got to get him out of here! We've got to take him somewhere and dump him! You understand? We've gotta, we've gotta . . .

Ruben (*simultaneously*)   We ransom him. We hold him ransom. We do this. We hold him ransom.

Benny   We . . . we *what*?

Beck   (*Pause.*) You mean . . . we kidnap him?

Moon   Oh Christ, Oh Christ . . .

Benny   Who do you think you are? Fu Man Fucking Chu? Master Criminal?

Moon (*simultaneously*)   Oh Jesus, Oh Christ . . .

Ruben   Moony. Stop it. Stop it. We're gonna be all right. No one knows he's here. He was on his own, he was pissed. It was just chance he came in here. He won't even remember coming in here. He won't even remember where he was. No one will ever know.

Benny   We can't do this.

Ruben   We have. It's that simple. We already have. We ransom him, we give some of the money to Landers – we're clear. No one ever knows. It's like a perfect crime . . . because we didn't plan it! It's just chance.

Pause.

Beck   How much . . . How much could we get?

Benny   What? What are you talking about – 'How much?'

Beck (*simultaneously*)   I'm just saying . . . if we did . . . how much would we ask for?

Ruben   Four thousand pounds.

Silence. They stare at him.

It's the Krays, isn't it? It's nothing to them.

Pause.

Benny   Four thousand pounds?

Ruben   Yeah. That's . . . Yeah. Think about that.

Pause.

Think about it, Benny. No more of this shit. You want to do this for the rest of your life? *Saucy Sally's Schoolgirl Secrets*? Moony wiping up old men's spunk?

Moon   Hey! Hey! I'm the door man!

Ruben   Do you mop up spunk? Yes or no?

Beat.

Moon   Yes – but I do other stuff as well . . .

Ruben   We do this, we get the money and we ride off into the sunset, Benny. You and me and Dorothy Lamour in the middle. Spend the rest of our lives lying in the sun. Maybe have a nice little chain of our own cinemas. Proper cinemas, showing proper films. No more protection money to the Goyim. This is your chance to be somebody.

Beck (*softly*)   Four thousand pounds.

Moon   That's . . . that's a thousand pounds each.

Benny   Four thousand pounds?

Ruben   Look at that.

They stare out to the audience.

Can you see that?

Moon   What?

Ruben   A happy ending.

They stare out. Music.

Scene Five

The back room. **Reg** *is tied to a chair, still blindfolded.* **Ruben** *stands close, wearing* **Reg**'s *coat.* **Reg** *stirs. Music stops.* **Ruben** *quickly steps away and puts the gun back in the pocket. Pause.*

Ruben   Would you like some tea?

Pause.

Ruben   I'm really sorry about your head.

Pause.

Do you want some ice or something?

Reg   What?

Ruben   For your head? Or can I get you any aspirin or anything?

Reg   Why don't you come over here and give me a big kiss, you love me so fucking much. Come over here and –

Ruben   Look, I know you must be pissed off –

Reg   Why the fuck would I be pissed off? Just 'cos some little wop puff hits me over the head, kidnaps me?

Ruben   That's not how I would describe this –

Reuben

Reg   I mean that might piss some people off, but I think –
it's Christmas – What the hell . . . Look, this is not (I'm sorry
about the head thing, that was . . I admit that was a mistake)
but this is not really a kidnapping.

Reg   This isn't a kidnapping?

Ruben   This is –

Reg   What the fuck is it? This is a date? Are we dating
now, Frankie?

Ruben   We need some money. (*Pause.*) We owe someone
some money. When you walked in, Mr Kray, that was . . .
well, that was like a sign. That was like a film or something –
like when Bogart turns up in *Key Largo* or something.
Someone . . . special . . . turning up. Changing things.
(*Pause.*) You're a twin, aren't you? (*Pause.*) I had a twin.

Pause.

Reg   You think I'm someone special, Frankie?

Ruben   Yes. I, uh, I, I do. I've read about you. The way
you just do things. The way you're not afraid. I'd like to . . .
I'd like to be like that. My dad, my real dad, was Italian
American. He was connected. He used to tell me all these
stories, about Capone or Luciano or Frankie Yale, like how
Yale was just fifteen when he got his bones? All of them,
they were just kids when they did it. And I think that . . .
that must mean something, mustn't it? Killing someone
when you're just a kid, that must . . . you know?

Pause.

Reg   What happened to your twin?

Ruben   He died. There was this fire . . . when we were
kids. This man . . . my stepdad . . . um . . .

Pause.

Reg   I want a fag.

Ruben *gives him a cigarette. As he lights it,* **Reg** *holds his wrist.*

Reg You wearing my coat?

Beat.

Ruben Yes.

Music.

Scene Six

Reg, **Moon** *and* **Beck** *sit playing cards.* **Benny** *and* **Ruben** *sit at another table .* **Beck**, **Moon** *and* **Benny** *wear sheets of paper pinned to them which read meany, miney and mo, respectively.*
Ruben *is on the phone, writing down a list of numbers.*

Benny . . . walking past a synagogue and they hear this long, drawn out wail. So the first Goy says, 'What's that noise?' Second Goy says 'That's just the Jews blowing their shofar.'

Ruben (*covering the mouth-piece*) Mo?

Benny So the first Goy says, 'Fuck me, those Jews know how to treat their help.'

Ruben Mo, could you . . . could you stop drinking?

Beck Fold.

Benny *takes the bottle and pours himself another large glass.*
Ruben *stares at him.*

Ruben (*to phone*) Yes, sorry. Go on.

Ruben *continues to write numbers down.*

Moon Your bet, Mr Kray. (*Beat.*) Oh yeah. Sorry. Hang on . . .

He moves behind **Reg** *and checks his cards for him. He whispers the result into* **Reg***'s ear then returns to his own seat. Pause.* **Reg** *sighs.*

Reg Raise you five.

Moon *takes the money from* **Reg**'s *pile and moves it to the middle of the table. He stares at his own cards. Pause.*

Ruben (*to phone*)   Uhuh . . .

Benny   Here's one for you. This little Christian boy gets murdered . . .

Ruben   Benny . . .

Benny   All the Jews are terrified. They know there'll be a pogrom. They get together in the Synagogue, trying to decide what to do. Suddenly the president of the synagogue runs in.

Ruben   Benny . . .

Benny   'Brothers,' he says, 'I've got wonderful news! The murdered boy is Jewish!'

Ruben   (*Beat.*) This isn't a joke.

Benny   No. No, it isn't.

Beck *is staring at* **Moon**.

Beck   Fuck me.

Moon   Do you mind? Do you . . .

Beck   Fuck me.

Moon   I'm deciding!

Beck   Deciding what, you prick? I've folded and you've just seen what he's got! What's there to fucking decide? Waste of –

Moon   I'm just . . . do I tell you how to play? We're enjoying it.

Beck   Waste of fucking time. How can he play cards when he can't see? Excuse me . . .

Moon   He's enjoying it!

Beck (*to* **Reg**)   Excuse me, are you enjoying this?

Reg   No.

Beck   There, see? He's not enjoying it.

Moon   We've got Scrabble, Mr Kray.

Beck   Oh, Jesus.

Moon   Am I talking to you?

Beck   He can't fucking see!

Moon   Am I . . . What? You can . . . you can feel the letters! It's like . . . like Braille or something!

Beck (*to* **Reg**)   Excuse me?

Moon   I'm not saying . . . I'm just saying we've got Scrabble.

Beck   Excuse me, Mr Kray, do you want to play scrabble?

Reg   Frankie?

Ruben   Yes, Mr Kray?

Reg   Do me a favour?

Ruben   Yes.

Reg   Kill me before these two cunts say one more word.

Beck (*to* **Beeny**)   Hey! Be . . . Um . . . (*He stops himself as* **Benny** *shoots him a warning glance.*) Well, what's your name! (**Benny** *shows him the sheet of paper pinned to his chest.*) Mo! He shouldn't be talking to us like that! This isn't the way we should be doing this. I mean, for a start, who plays cards with the fucking kidnappee?

Benny   With the . . . what? Kidnappee?

Beck   It's what you call them! And he shouldn't be out here with –

Benny   What the fuck is a kidnappee?

Beck   Look I can't help it if you know nowt about this stuff. When I was doing time –

Benny   Oh, here we go. Al Capone's Memoirs.

Beck   When I was doing time, there was this bloke who
was in for kidnapping. He told me all about it. It's . . . I
mean . . . there's like rules and that. If we're gonna do it, we
should be doing it properly. And we should have guns.

Moon   You what?

Beck   I'm saying, we should have guns. For protection.
We should be doing this properly! When I was doing
time . . .

Benny (*to* **Ruben**)   How many Krays have you found?

Ruben   (*Beat.*) Forty-five.

Benny   Forty-five. (*Beat.*) You're going to ring them all?
On my phone bill? I'm gonna be the only kidnapper in
history who loses money on the deal.

Beck   Is anyone listening to me?

Ruben   Mr Kray? We . . . We could do with a hand here.
I'm asking you again. Please. What's your brother's phone
number?

Reg   You haven't exactly put a lot of thought into this job,
have you, Frankie? I have to say, I feel a little insulted.

Ruben   Please, Mr Kray – just the number.

Reg   Frankie, Frankie. Me – The kidappee – is not
expected to cooperate with the kidnappers. That's your
basic rule. (*To* **Beck**.) Didn't your bum chum inside tell you
that?

Ruben   But this is – this isn't helpful . . . this is . . . this . . .

Moon   We could torture him.

They all stare at him.

I mean – I just – Sorry, Mr Kray. It just came out. But I
mean – it would save time, wouldn't it?

Reg   Pardon me, Miney. I haven't known you for long. I mean, to me you're just a bloke in something furry, so I'm guessing here – but it strikes me that you are possibly not the best person to talk about torturing me – on account of you being the stupidest cunt I have ever come across.

Beck   Hoy! Can we . . . Can we just remember who's in charge here?

Reg   Sorry – the second stupidest cunt I have ever come across.

Beck   Is that . . . are you talking about me?

Ruben   Meany! Will you sit down!

Beck   No! I've had enough of this! Are you fucking talking to –

Benny (*to* **Beck**)   Hey! Shmendrick! Sit down! Take the weight off your balls. No one's torturing anyone. There are ways of behaving, ways of conducting your self in business. What you do – to get what you want, that's what counts. That's how you show who you . . .

Beck *crosses to* **Reg** *and produces a knife. He holds it to* **Reg**'s *throat.*

Beck   Ten seconds to tell me the number or I kill you. Ten – nine . . .

Benny   What?

Moon   Oh Christ.

Beck   Eight – seven . . .

Ruben   Put it down!

Beck   Fuck off! Six – five . . .

Benny   Wait a minute! Wait a minute!

Ruben *crosses to* **Beck** *and pulls a gun out of the coat pocket. He holds it to* **Beck**'s *head.*

Ruben   I said put it down.

Pause. Everybody freezes. Slowly **Beck** *lowers the knife and puts it on the table.*

Moon   Frankie? Frankie?

Pause. **Ruben** *lowers the gun. Shaken,* **Beck** *crosses to the others.*

Reg   You got my gun, Frankie?

Ruben   Yes.

Reg   I thought you might have. Why should I help you, Frankie?

Pause.

Ruben   I . . . I don't know. (*Beat.*) My twin . . .

Reg   What?

Benny   Frankie . . . ?

Ruben   My twin . . . he died . . . there was a fire . . . my step . . . the man who brought me up . .

Benny   Frankie! Shut up!

Ruben   He set fire to the house . . . they said it was an accident but . . . (*Pause.*) They got me out. My brother died. (*Pause.*) When I met you . . . it was like . . .

Pause.

Reg   That gun's killed men. You think you can do that? Do you know what you can do? Eh?

Ruben   I . . . I don't know what you mean.

Reg   I'm talking about belief, Frankie. Belief in what you can do. Yeah? In what you are. What you're capable of. You want me to help you. Show me how much.

Ruben   How much?

Reg   Like an initiation. Yeah?

Pause.

Ruben   What do I have to do?

Reg   You got my little case? Bring me my little case.

Ruben *brings the small suitcase to him.*

Reg   Open it.

Ruben *opens the case.*

Reg   Tell me what's in there.

Ruben   Fingers. It's full of fingers.

Reg   Yeah. (*Beat.*) Little sacrifices. (*Beat.*) Show me how much belief you've got Frankie. Make a little sacrifice for me.

Pause. **Ruben** *holds up the knife and puts his hand on the table.*

Benny   Frankie? What . . . what are you doing?

Moon   Frankie?

Benny   Put it down! Frankie! Put it . . .what the . . .what the fuck do you think you are doing?

Pause. **Ruben** *cuts off the first finger of his left hand.*

Benny   NO!

Moon   Frigging hell . . . I'm gonna be sick . . .

Shaking, **Ruben** *gives the finger to* **Reg**. *Pause.*

Reg   Ring 56732, at noon tomorrow. Tell them how much you want. If they ask for proof. You send them your finger with this ring on it.

He takes of his ring and drops it on the table.

Ruben   Miney? Miney?

Moon   Yeah.

Ruben   Write it down. 56732. Write that down.

Moon *writes.*

Ruben   You done it?

Moon   Yeah.

Silence.

Ruben (*weakly*)   I didn't think . . .

Reg   What?

Ruben   I didn't think you'd really let me do it.

Music. Blackout.

Act Two

Scene One

Early the next morning. The back room. **Ruben** *has a bandage on his left hand and the gun in the right. As the lights rise* **Ruben** *is aiming the gun at* **Reg** *who sits without his blindfold on.* **Ruben** *is still wearing* **Reg***'s coat. Pause.* **Ruben** *lowers the gun.*

Reg Did it give you a hard-on?

Ruben (*Beat.*) No.

Reg *considers.*

Reg Well, doesn't always work. What did you feel?

Ruben (*Beat.*) Scared.

Reg Tell you what it is, right? You're going to do a thing, and you feel as if something inside you can't do it . . . like it's a wrong thing . . . ?

Ruben Yes.

Reg But how do you know that thing inside you is right? How do you know that's even part of you and not something *they* put in you, from when you was a nipper? That's the problem.

Ruben Yes.

Reg There are rules. But whose rules Frankie? That's your problem.

Ruben Yes. This is . . . yes.

Reg This is the truth, right?

Ruben Right.

Reg There aren't any rules. There are no rules.

Ruben Right.

Reg   There's no good, no bad . . . there's just what you do.
Yes? And that is what you are.

Ruben   Yes. (*Pause.*) I just can't seem to . . . I can't . . .

Reg   (*Beat.*) You've got it all bottled up in you, haven't
you.

Ruben   What?

Reg   I can tell. It's not good for you, Frankie. Gotta get it
out.

Ruben   Get it . . .

Reg   You know what I'm talking about. I can feel it
between you and the others. Lot of hate there.

Ruben   Hate? No . . . Not . . . We're like a family. It's like
between you and Ronnie.

Reg   Ronnie?

Ruben   Your . . . brother? Ronnie?

Reg   Let me tell you this . . . Hate. Hate keeps you clean. I
know you know what I'm talking about. Yeah? Who do you
hate?

Ruben   I don't think I do.

Reg   Yes, you do. You do. I can feel it. You got a little
voice in your head, telling you it's wrong. Against the rules.
(*Beat.*) Who do you hate?

Ruben   I don't . . .

Reg   Fuck the little voice! You keep listening to that voice,
you're gonna bottle all this up in you, come sixty-five you're
gonna be in bed with the missus, she's says 'Do you fancy a
cuppa love?' and you're gonna stab her in the neck with the
table lamp. It happens all the time. Filth asks you why you
did it, happily married old bloke like you? You're gonna say
'The devil made me do it.' Happens all the time. Well,
there's no devil. You just kept it in you too long. That's why

society's so fucked up. People fucking animals and that . . .
they just don't know what to do. Is that their fault? Society,
right, hasn't let them live. Do you read, Frankie?

Ruben   I . . .

Reg   I read. I read a lot of history. You should read
history. Times past right, Olde England, right, people
wanted to do something, kill someone, whatever, they just
do it. They don't worry about it's right or wrong, yeah?
They just do it. True. Kings and Queens? Fucking
bloodbath. The way we're meant to be. You ever try to top
yourself Frankie?

Ruben   I . . .

Reg   Course you have. 'Cos you're fucked up. Don't be
ashamed. It's not your fault. I tried to top myself once, long
time ago. Same thing. All that hate and you're not letting it
out? Stands to reason it's gonna poison you. History, right?
Did you know the Ancient Greeks didn't have a word for
topping themselves? I read that. Didn't know what it meant.
Never did it. Why? 'Cos Mr Greek sees someone who's a
cunt, he doesn't keep it to himself, doesn't think it's wrong,
Mr Greek goes up to the aforementioned cunt and
introduces the cunt to his club. Wallop. He just does it.
Doesn't go to confession after. Wallop. That's for being such
a cunt. You know your Ancient Greeks never fucked
animals. That's a fact. Put these two things together. I'm
telling you Frankie . . . let it out. Before you go bad. (*Beat.*)
Who do you hate? Tell me who you hate, Frankie.

Ruben   I don't . . .

Reg   WHO DO YOU HATE?

Ruben (*long pause*)   Jews. I hate the Jews.

Reg   There. Feels better doesn't it?

Ruben   Yes.

Reg   Say it again.

Ruben   I hate Jews.

Reg   There. Feel better?

Ruben   Yes.

Reg   Good. (*Beat.*) Beautiful gun, innit?

Ruben   Yes.

Reg   Beautiful guns, Lugers. You know who used those?

Ruben   Who?

Reg   SS. SS gun that. Beautifully made.

Pause. **Ruben** *stares at the gun.*

Reg   Think about that, Frankie. Think about where that gun's been. Eh? That's history there. You think of who that gun's done. History in your hands. (*Pause.*) You go out this morning.

Ruben   (*Beat.*) Yes. (*Beat.*) I went to check the papers. See if you were in them.

Reg   (*Beat.*) Was I?

Ruben *takes a folded paper out of the coat pocket. He tosses it onto* **Reg**'s *lap.* **Reg** *stares at the front page then rips it from the rest of the paper.*

Reg   One for the scrap book.

He folds the sheet and puts it in his trouser pocket. Suddenly **Ruben** *raises the gun again and aims at his head.* **Reg** *stares calmly back at him. He reaches out and casually checks* **Ruben**'s *groin.*

Reg   Now you've got it.

Ruben *lowers the gun.* **Reg** *laughs.*

Scene Two

The projection room. **Moon** *and* **Beck** *are watching* Key Largo. *We hear Bogart speaking in the film.*

Beck . . . but that's it. *That is it!* Fuck them. I've stuck by them, I've . . . you can't say I . . . everyone telling me I was mad, I was fuckin' mad. Been running this place on me own! Think I'm gonna sit here, with this going on, I mean, biggest thing in your life, and that little fucking, fucking yid thinking he's telling *me* what to do, with his fuckin' gun . . . I nearly . . . (*Beat.*) Fuckin' Jews for you.

Moon What?

Beck Crack under pressure, don't they?

Moon Do they?

Beck Course they do. Friggin' nutter. Cutting off his own finger. I was this close to having him. I'm telling you. Thing about Jews right, they can't handle the pressure. (*Beat.*) You can't argue with that.

Pause.

Moon What about *The Vikings*?

Beck What?

Moon Kirk Douglas in *The Vikings*.

Beck What?

Moon Well, he gets his eye pecked out and that and it doesn't even bother him. He's jumping over oars and all sorts.

Beck What the fuck has Kirk Douglas got to do with it?

Moon Well, he's a Jew.

Beck What?

Moon And this bird pecks his eye out and he just gets this patch thing and . . .

Beck   Kirk Douglas is fucking american, you fucking wanker!

Moon   He's a Jew. I read it.

Beck   Right. Just shut up. Shut up. I don't even want to talk to you any more.

Pause.

Moon   And Tony Curtis is in *The Vikings*.

Beck   Shut up!

Pause.

Moon   And he gets his hand cut off and that and he . . .

Beck   Moony, I'm gonna fucking belt you! (*Pause.*) If you had a fucking brain you'd understand what I'm trying to tell you!

Moon   What are you trying to tell me?

Beck   I'm trying to tell you that the thing about Jews is –

Benny *enters. He turns off the projector.*

Benny   Thing about Jews is they pay the wages of Goys like you.

Moon   Hiya, Benny.

Benny   What time is it?

Moon   Half nine.

Benny   Half nine in the morning and you two drinking already. Fucking animals. Give me that!

He takes the bottle and takes a long drink from it.

I must have blacked out. All this going on and I fall asleep.

Moon   It's the shock. Like me dad. He said in the war, before they went on a raid, he would fall asleep.

Benny   Right. Your dad a pilot?

Moon   Cook.

Benny   Right. Where's Ruben?

Moon   He's gone to get some food. He said he wanted to check the papers. Just in case.

Beck   Tell him, what you heard.

Benny   What did you hear?

Moon   Nothing. It was just. Last night. After you went to sleep. I heard Ruben and Mr Kray talking in the backroom.

Benny   Talking about what?

Moon   I dunno, the door was closed.

Beck   Well, I don't know about you two but he's making me nervous. He is making me very nervous. How do we know he's not sorting out some deal with Kray. Eh? Little private arrangement? Having their little kiss and cuddle, making the wedding plans.

Benny   Shut up, Beck.

Beck   Yeah, shut up, Beck. You know. You know I'm right. Fucking weirdo. Cutting off his finger.

Benny *sits down.*

Pause.

Moon   How'd you sleep?

Benny   Terrible. Kept dreaming about little Izzy.

Beck   Who?

Benny   Ruben's twin. Fucking horrible dream.

Moon   So – was that true, Benny? About your dad and the fire and that?

Benny   Ruben doesn't know what he's talking about. My father brought him up like he was one of his own. How many men would do that, eh? Come home from the war

and find their veib up the stick with some goy's twins.
Anyone else would have thrown them all out. It was an
accident, is all. A cigarette. What can you say? It's a terrible
world.

Moon   Poor little bairn.

Beck   Were you there?

Benny   No. I was staying at a friend's.

Beck   Right.

Beat.

Benny   What's that mean?

Beck   What?

Benny   What's the 'right' mean.

Beck   It means right.

Benny   I asked to go there, OK? It was a coincidence.

Beck   Hey, calm down, Benny. No one's arguing.

Benny   Ruben's always been like that. Always wants
someone to blame for life. If only he had a twin, if only he
wasn't a Jew, and if he was a goy it would be if only he was
a Jew. All right – so we didn't fit in when we were kids.
Things were rough. What do you want? You think the
world owes you a hug?

He takes a big drink.

Fucking mess. Woke up this morning, I swear to God, I had
to stop myself just going out the door, keeping on going.

Moon   Why didn't you?

Benny   This is all I've got. Ruben, this dump. It's all I've
got.

Beck   We all want this to work, Benny. We've got
everything riding on this. But Ruben . . . Ruben shouldn't

be in charge of this any more. Someone's got to take over. Someone with more experience of this stuff.

Benny   Like you, for instance?

Beck   Yes, like me. It's about time people started taking me seriously. I've done stuff. I know people. I can get us through this.

Benny   Listen, Beck – don't waste my time with this, OK?

Beck   You know I'm right.

Benny   I don't know. I don't know anything any more – except this – you are not a gangster. You are a schmuck. We are schmucks. We are life's schmucks who have somehow – some fucking how ended up in this mess – but don't go thinking you have the ability to do anything about it, OK?

Beck   What are you saying? You're saying you don't think I can do it?

Benny   OH, STOP IT WILL YOU? You're nothing! OK? You're nothing. And that's fine. I like it in a man. I'm nothing myself. Just don't go mistaking yourself for someone, all right?

Beck (*quietly*)   Fuck you, Benny.

Benny   *Nu?* Truth hurts, boynik.

Beck   Fuck you. Fuck you and your brother.

Ruben *enters*.

Beck   Speak of the devil.

Moon   Hiya, Ruben. How's your hand, mate? How's your . . . um . . . your finger?

Beck   How's his finger. Tit! It's in a fucking envelope!

Moon   Sorry, Abe, I just meant . . . Did you get anything to eat?

Ruben   What?

Moon   Did you get any food?

Ruben   No. No . . . I forgot.

Benny   Did you check the papers?

Ruben   Yeah.

Benny   And?

Ruben   And what?

Benny   Is there anything in them? About Kray?

Ruben   No.

Benny   You're sure?

Ruben   I just fucking said so, didn't I? (*Pause.*) Listen, I've come to a decision. I've talked about our situation, about Landers, with Mr Kray and –

Benny   What?

Beck   You what?

Ruben   And I've decided. Landers' not getting the money.

Benny   He's not . . . He's not . . . He's what?

Beck   You talked to Kray?

Ruben   What is this about? What has this all been about?

Benny   What has this . . .Getting the money! Getting the fucking money to pay back Landers.

Ruben   No! No – the money's nothing. People who just want the money – they're . . . they don't understand anything! This is about being . . . Men . . . being Men Acting in the world, you know? Acting and . . . Believing. Landers he . . . he can't touch that. He can't hurt us.

Benny   Landers can't hurt us?

Ruben   He doesn't have belief.

Benny   No, you're right. He probably doesn't have belief.
He does, however, have a great big shotgun which he is
happy to shove up your arse, pull the trigger – give you a
centre parting. Hurt? I don't know. But this, I think, would
smart a little.

Moon   I don't understand . . . I don't . . .

Beck   Right, now you listen to me. Forget the Landers
thing. I'm more concerned about you getting too attached
to your new boyfriend.

Ruben   What?

Beck   You heard. 'I've come to a decision. Big man with
your gun. There's four of us in this and I don't remember
voting you Chief.

Moon   Beck . . .

Beck   What? Beck, what? Can I talk? Can I air my
fucking opinions. I mean, excuse me, but I seem to
remember that this goes wrong I get killed too.

Ruben   No one is getting hurt. He gave us the number,
didn't he? You saw that with the finger . . . he knows I'm . . .
I've got belief – like him. So – no one's getting hurt.

Beck   Right. And before you ask – when I say 'right' I
mean 'fuck you sideways no one's getting hurt'.

Moon   Beck.

Beck   Fuck off, Moon. What are you – his mother?

Ruben   All right, Beck. I'm sick of this. Let's sort this out.
You've got worries – what are they?

Beck   Worries? Yes – I have worries. I worry that
suddenly our kidnap victim is your long-lost blood brother. I
worry that you're cutting off your frigging finger because he
asks you to. I worry that you're telling him your lovely tales
from a fucked-up childhood and that next you'll be giving
him our names and addresses in case he wants to become

our pen pal for life. And I'm worried that I'm going to get to meet little barbecued Izzy in person.

Silence. **Ruben** *takes out the gun. He points it at* **Beck***. Tension. Slowly he lowers the gun. Pause.*

Ruben   What's that staring thing? Don't stare at me, Benny?

Benny *stares at him in silence. Then looks away.* **Ruben** *walks out.*

Beck   Tell me I'm wrong now, Benny. Tell me I'm wrong.

Music.

Scene Three

Reg *and* **Ruben** *in the back room.*

Reg   You like the porn movies, then?

Ruben   Not really. I like the old movies.

Reg   Yeah? Why you show them, then?

Ruben   It's what people want to see.

Reg   (*Beat.*) I saw one once, that this bloke had made of his missus and a dog. You do anything like that?

Ruben   No.

Reg   (*Beat.*) Border Collie it was. Border Collie? The black and white one's?

Ruben   Yes.

Reg   Yeah. Friendly dogs. (*Beat.*) Well this one fuckin' was, anyway.

Pause.

Reg   What's the matter with you?

Ruben   Nothing. I'm tired. I haven't slept. I'm just . . . tired.

Reg   So have a kip.

Ruben   Yeah. I will. When things are sorted. (*Beat.*) I . . . I nearly did it. Before. I nearly killed someone. And I didn't. I was scared.

Reg   Yeah?

Ruben   I still couldn't . . . I couldn't . . . (*Pause.*) What's it . . . what's it *like*?

Reg   Yeah. They always want know about that.

Ruben   I'm sorry.

Reg   People always want to ask you about that. Wanna know what it's like.

Ruben   I'm sorry.

Reg   (*Beat.*) You wanna know what it feels like? Well I'll tell you, right? 'Cos it's a funny thing. Now, you might not understand this, but I'm telling you, every time you kill someone you feel a bit, sort of . . . lighter. I can't explain that, but it's true. You just feel, sort of lighter.

Ruben   Like you're free.

Reg   Like you're free.

Ruben   Because you've got belief.

Reg   That's it. That's right. Belief. You know what I'm talking about. I think we've got a lot in common, Ruben.

Ruben   I feel that way, Mr Kray. (*Pause.*) I was wondering . . .

Reg   What?

Ruben   Nothing, sorry. Sounds stupid.

Reg   What have we been talking about here, Frankie? Don't worry what something's going to sound like – just say it. Men don't hide stuff from each other.

Ruben   It's just, I was wondering, after this is over, when you're back in London . . . Could I come and see you?

Reg   Come and see me?

Ruben   Could we . . . could we do stuff together, do you think?

Reg   You mean work together?

Ruben   I . . . yes, that's what I'd like. I could be like an apprentice.

Reg   I don't know, Frankie.

Ruben   No . . . I know . . . it's stupid . . .

Reg   It's just . . . we're quite a tight outfit, you know?

Ruben   I know, I shouldn't have asked . . .

Reg   No, I'm not saying that. You know, I've got to admit, I feel . . . like a connection here . . .

Ruben   That's what I feel, too. I do. It's like a . . it sounds stupid . . . but it's like a brother thing . . . don't you think?

Reg   There'd be certain tests – you understand that? There'd be things you'd have to be able to do.

Ruben   Like . . . like getting my bones?

Reg   Well, yes. That would be one thing.

Ruben   I understand that! That's what I want. I want to test myself.

Reg   Well, who knows. Maybe we could do some stuff together. Obviously I can't promise . . .

Ruben   Of course . . . really . . . that's . . . thank you.

Reg   That's OK.

Ruben   Thank you.

Reg   OK.

Ruben   Do you think Ronnie will like me?

Reg   Ronnie? (*Beat.*) Oh yeah. Ronnie'll love you.

Pause. **Ruben** *takes off* **Reg***'s blindfold.*

Ruben   Mr Kray? There's something I have to tell you. I have lied to you. I'm not Italian. I wanted to be. I made up this thing about my mam telling me my dad was Italian. I have this memory of her saying that – I really do – but I think . . . I think she didn't. I don't want there to be any lies between us any more. I mean . . . what's it matter, any way? Who you were born? It's not worth lying about, is it? (*Pause.*) My name's Ruben Stein. I'm a Jew.

Pause.

Reg   I understand.

Ruben   Do you?

Reg   Yeah. I understand. (*Beat.*) It doesn't matter who you were born, son.

Ruben   Thank you.

Reg   You feel better?

Ruben   Yes.

Reg   Good. I'm starving. You got any food?

Ruben   I'll go and get you something.

He starts to go.

Reg   Ruben?

Ruben   Yes, Mister Kray?

Reg   What's do you call Jew food again? Kosher?

Ruben   Yes.

Reg   Get me something Kosher, yeah?

Ruben   Really?

Reg   Yeah. I'll try that.

Ruben (*happily*)   All right Mister Kray.

Benny *enters.*

Benny   Frankie, can I . . . ?

*He sees that **Reg** has no blindfold on.*

Ruben (*to* **Reg**)   Thanks for everything, Mr Kray.

Reg   That's OK, Ruben.

Benny   Um . . . Frankie? Can I . . . Can I have a quick word? Could you come here, please?

Ruben *joins him.*

Beeny   What did he just call you?

Ruben   It's OK . . .

Benny   Where's the fucking blindfold? How does he know your name?

Ruben   You don't have to worry about that any more, Benny.

Benny   What the fuck are you doing?

Ruben   Mr Kray and I have had a talk and we've agreed that . . . well . . . it's too soon to say, but there's a possibility that we might be working together. So you don't have to worry about the names or any of that stuff any more. We're like one big family now. OK? (*Pause.*) Here.

*He gives **Benny** the gun.*

I'm gonna go out and get some food. You better hang on to that for me. I'll be back before twelve.

Ruben *walks out.* **Benny** *stares ahead.*

Reg   So? How you doing, Benny?

Scene Four

Moon, **Benny** *and* **Beck** *sit in front of the back-room door. The gun is on the table before them.* **Benny** *is drinking and playing cards with* **Moon***.*

Beck   What time is it?

Moon (*rapidly*)   And, I mean, everyone needs to settle down sometime, don't they? Nice house and that, and holidays and that, and and she's the one for me, I'm telling you. First thing I'm gonna do. Settle down. We've been looking at prams.

Benny   What do you want?

Moon   Twist. You've seen her, haven't you, Benny?

Benny   Who?

Moon   Debbie. At the fancy-dress party. Last month. Jimmy's.

Beck   What time is it?

Benny   Eleven thirty. (*To* **Moon**.) Who was she?

Moon   Wilma.

Benny   Wilma?

Moon   Flintstone. Cave-girl thing.

Benny   Right. What do you want?

Beck   So we've got maybe twenty minutes.

Moon   There's something different about her. She's really quiet and she doesn't swear. She's got this fucking amazing smile and – I mean – I know she comes from Blyth . . .

Benny   What do you want?

Moon   I don't know. Byker would be better. Blyth's fucking miles.

Benny   No, Moon. The cards – what do you want?

Moon   Oh, Um . . . Twist.

Beck   Twenty minutes.

Moon   And we talk a lot – I mean she's really intelligent.
And she's not stuck-up at all. She knows load of stuff but she
doesn't show off – and she's always buying us presents –
clothes, watches and that.

Benny   Tits?

Moon   Flat.

Beck   Twenty minutes

Benny   I always fancied Betty Flintstone.

Moon   Rubble. Betty's married to Barney.

Benny   Right. What do you want?

Moon   Twist. I'm telling you, I could do a lot worse – a lot
worse.

Beck   Hello? Hello?

Benny   What do you want?

Moon   Twist. Fuck, bust.

Benny   How much?

Moon   Forty-two.

Benny   So close. Perhaps if you tried to . . .

Beck   I said . . .

Benny   We heard what you said!

Beck   Then can we cut out the Spring Bride shit and talk
for a second here?

Pause.

Moon   What you going to do with your money, Beck?

Pause.

Beck?

Beck We've got twenty minutes then Old Frankie comes back and things get a little bit more difficult. Now, if we're gonna get the job done, then I say we take charge of this outfit and we do this thing now. He comes back. It's done. What's he going to do? We collect the money. We're safe. We're home. Ruben can sulk in the corner. But we have to do this thing now.

Benny This thing? What's this? We're in a fucking film now? What's this thing? Say it.

Beck Don't fucking start with me, Benny.

Benny Say it. You want us to do something, have the decency to say it like it is.

Beck Kill him. (*Pause.*) All right? There . . . I've said it. We have to kill him. And you know that's the truth.

Moon What? What the fuck's he talking about? Kill him? Tell him, Benny.

Beck You know it, Benny. Ruben's mad as fuck. He's gonna let Kray go – he's gonna – fuck knows – he's gonna tell him our names – fuck knows – he's off the rails. New Year's Day, we wake up dead. We've got to kill him.

Moon Right. Fine. That's good. Kidnapping Reggie Kray. I wasn't very happy about that. I thought that might piss his brother off a bit. But killing him, no, really, that's fine. That's not going to piss anyone off, is it?

Pause.

Hello? Hello? Why isn't anybody talking here? What, what? You're considering this, Benny? You're considering the words of this fucking lunatic? (No offence, Beck.) We've been through this. We've agreed on this.

Benny Ruben took the blindfold off him and told him his real name. And he called me Benny in front of him.

Pause.

Beck   Did he tell him our names?

Benny   I don't know. Maybe.

Beck   OK. I take it that settles it. We kill him. Only way we get off the hook.

Moon   We get off the hook? We kill Reg Kray and you think that gets us off the hook? I say that gets us on to a bigger hook. I say that gets us on to the biggest hook they can fit up your arse.

Pause. **Benny** *stares at* **Beck**.

Benny   He's right. We kill him.

Moon   What? What? What?

Benny   You think I'm happy about this? You think I want to do this? We don't have a choice any more!

Moon   No, Benny! No! Please. We could run!

Beck   What about the money?

Moon   Fuck the money!

Benny   Where you going to hide, Moon? There's nowhere you can go they won't find you. It's what they do.

Moon   Please, Benny . . . please . . .

Benny   I know, Moon! I know! It makes me feel sick to my stomach but I . . . I don't know another way. It's us or him. That's it. That's all there is.

Pause.

Moon   All I wanted . . . I just thought . . . Ruben said we would be rich and I could have a house and that and settle down. You know what I mean? I don't want be a fucking film star or anything. I just wanted to settle down. Have a bairn and that. We've been looking at prams, you know.

Beck   Yeah. But you see, don't you?

Miserably **Moon** *nods his head.*

Beck   All right. We cut the cards to see who does it.

Moon   What? No way! No Fucking Way! No fucking way am I doing it!

Beck   Fucking kids. Like working with fucking kids!

Moon   Hey, Old Man River! You want to be the grown-up? You want to be the Man? You do it!

Beck   We cut the cards! It's the only fair way!

Moon   Benny?

Benny   None of us want to do it.

Pause.

Beck   OK. Moon – cut the pack.

Moon   Why've I got to go first?

Beck   Oh, fuck's sake!

Benny   All right! I'll go first. Lowest card does it.

Benny *cuts the cards. A high number.* **Beck** *cuts next. Another high number. Pause.* **Moon** *cuts. A low number. Pause.* **Beck** *takes out a knife and puts it on the table in front of* **Moon**.

Moon   What about best of three?

Beck   Yes. Why not? Then we can have paper, scissors, stone. Then we can play fucking patty cake for it!

Pause. **Moon** *stares at the knife.*

Moon   Benny? I don't think I can do this. I don't think I can kill someone.

Beck   Course you can, Moon. It's just like carving chicken.

Moon   I don't like chicken.

Beck   Fucking beef then! Listen, what you've got remember is you're not killing a nice man. You're killing a very nasty man who's done some very nasty things to people. You killing him is gonna please a lot of people. Widows and kids and stuff. Ok?

Moon   It's just – It's just blood and – I mean, you know how I am with blood and . . .

Beck   For fuck's sake!

Moon   No – No – Listen. It's a medical thing, isn't it, Benny? Benny knows – It's a medical thing, isn't it?

Beck   What the fuck are you talking about?

Moon   Blood and that – fainting – it's not that I'm scared, it's medical – like some people are with spiders – me mam worked in a butcher's . . .

Beck   I'll tell you what then, Moony. Why don't you just go in and talk to him? Why don't you just go in and whine at him and with a bit of luck he'll kill himself . . .

Benny   This is crazy! This is fucking crazy!

Beck   All right! All right! Moon. Listen. No one's gonna make you do this. All right? I know you didn't ask to be in this. But you want to be a Man – you want to do your bit to get us all out of this – you want to get your thousand pounds and settle down with Mrs Flintstone – you want to do something with your life – you want to be someone – then you do this. You want to be no one – you want to spend your life looking over your shoulder, never sure when your last day is – you want to leave us here to deal with this alone – then you get up and walk away. Leave here – don't come back – you're free – no one's going to blame you. (*Pause.*) The choice is yours, Moon. The choice is yours.

Moon   Right.

He gets up to leave.

Beck   Hoy! Where the fuck are you going? Sit down!

Moon   You said . . .

Beck   I lied! Sit down!

Moon *sits down again.*

Beck   Now you are going to do this thing. Do you understand? You are going to fucking do this.

Moon *stares at the knife.*

Moon (*imploring*)   Benny?

Benny *looks away. Pause.* **Moon** *stands up. He picks up the knife. He moves towards the back-room door.*

Beck   Moony? This is . . . we won't forget this. You're doing the right thing. I'm proud of you. And you know what – when this is done I'm gonna give you a new name – like . . . um . . . like Razor . . . or Blade . . .

Moon   Beck?

Beck   Yes, Moon?

Moon   Shut the fuck up, will you?

Beck   Absolutely. Not another word. You're the best.

Moon *stops at the back-room door.*

Moon   Can I use the gun?

Beck   Get in!

Moon *goes into the back room. Silence. Both men stare at each other.*

Beck   When Ruben comes back, we stand together on this, yes? And no fucking way does he get the gun back. And if he starts any trouble then –

Benny   Don't talk to me, Beck.

Beck   Hey! Don't go blaming me for this!

Benny   A man is about to die. Have a little respect.

Beck   Hey! I'm not happy about this either!

Benny   Aren't you? Isn't this what you wanted? I fucking know you! This will really give you something to brag about now, won't it? Big fucking gangster. Getting someone else to do your dirty work!

Beck   Fuck you! I could have done it! It was the cards!

Benny *heads for the back room.*

Beck   What you doing?

Benny   I'm stopping him! It's not right! We can't do . . .

Suddenly we hear a muffled moan from the storeroom. Both men stare at the door.

Beck   Do you think . . . ?

Benny   Yeah. I think. Oh, God. What have we done? It shouldn't have been Moon. It's not right.

Beck   We cut the cards! It was all fair and square!

Benny   It shouldn't have been him! He's like a little kid. . .

Beck   I didn't see you volunteering!

The door opens and **Moon** *comes slowly out he has blood on his hand and some on his face. Pause.*

Benny   Moon?

Beck   You're the Man, Moony. You're the fucking Man.

Moon *sits at the table.*

Beck   All went smoothly, yeah? All sorted?

Moon   I was looking at him . . . and . . . I think . . .

Beck   It's always hard the first time, son. Don't let it get to you.

Moon   I feel sick.

Benny (*to* **Beck**)   Oh, now with the advice. Now with the kibitz.

Moon   I think I'm gonna be sick.

Benny   Have you ever killed anyone?

Beck   What?

Benny   I'm asking you, boynik. Have you ever killed anyone?

Moon   I think . . .

Benny   Always hard the first time. Like you'd know. You fucking piece of shit!

Beck   Fuck you! I'm comforting him!

Benny   'You're the Man, Moony! You're the Man!' You wouldn't know a man if he stuck his finger up your arse! You think this is something to be proud of?

Moon   I think one of you is going to have to kill him.

Pause.

Beck   What?

Benny   What are you talking about, Moon? He . . . he isn't dead?

Moon   No. I told you I couldn't. I fainted.

Beck   You what?

Moon   I always do. I told you.

Beck   But the . . . the blood!

Moon (*noticing the blood*)   Oh, God. I must have banged me head. I feel sick.

Benny   Moon! Moon! The knife. Where's the knife?

Moon   I dunno. Must still be in there. I dropped it when I . . . (*Pause.*) Oh.

Reg *appears at the door – untied and without the blindfold.*

Reg   Hello, girls.

Silence. They stare at him in horror. **Beck** *grabs the gun and points it at* **Reg***.*

Beck   Put your hands up! PU-PUT YOUR HANDS UP!

Reg   (*Beat.*) Stick 'em up.

Beck   *What?*

Reg   You're supposed to say 'Stick 'em up.' I thought you girls watched the movies?

Beck   Shut up! Empty your pockets!

Reg   Make your fuckin' mind up. Which do you . . . ?

Beck   EMPTY YOUR POCKETS!

Reg *smiles and pulls his trouser pockets inside out. As he does so the folded sheet of newspaper falls to the floor. Nobody notices.*

Beck   Where is it? Where's the knife?

Reg   What? This knife?

He pulls a knife out from the back of his waistband. **Beck** *flinches.* **Reg** *smiles.*

Reg   Jumpy little cunt aren't you? I don't need a knife for you, do I, Dolores?

Beck   Put it down.

Reg   All I gotta do is fart loud enough and you'll die of a fuckin' heart attack.

Beck   PUT THE KNIFE DOWN!

Reg   (*Beat.*) Tell you what?

He drops the knife and spreads his arms wide.

How's that? One free shot. How's that, then?

Beck   You . . . you fucking . . . you think I won't do it? Do you? You think I can't do it? Do you?

Pause.

Benny   Beck?

Beck   No!

Pause. **Beck** *moves closer to* **Reg** *and aims the gun at his head.*

Benny   Beck?

Beck   SHUT UP! (*Pause. To* **Reg**.) You're nothing! (*Pause.*)
You're nothing!

He aims the gun again with both hands. Slowly **Benny** *crosses to
him.*

Beck   I can . . .

Benny *puts his hands on* **Beck**'*s shoulders.*

Benny   OK. OK.

Beck   I can . . . I can . . . do it . . .

Benny   I know you can.

Beck   He's nothing. I can do it.

Benny   OK. That's enough.

Beck *lowers the gun.*

That's enough.

Beck   I could do it, Benny. I could.

Benny   I know, Beck. I know you can. But I don't want
you to. We'll find another way. I don't know . . . I don't
know what we'll do . . . but we'll find another way. Yeah?
What are we, eh? We're not . . . we're not animals here.

Ruben *is standing in the doorway. He holds a bag of food.*

Moon (*seeing him*)   Benny?

Ruben *walks towards them. Silence. He takes the gun from* **Beck**.
Pause.

Moon   Ruben? I know this looks bad but but but if you
just let us . . . we have had a bit of a thing here.

Pause. **Ruben** *puts the gun in his pocket. He crosses to* **Reg** *and picks up the knife from the floor.*

Ruben   Are you all right, Mr Kray?

Reg   No. I'm fucking starving.

Ruben *stares at* **Benny**.

Benny   You going to shoot me now, Ruben? Go ahead. I don't give a fuck.

Ruben   Why Benny? Why would you try and do something like that? Why would you try and ruin everything like that? You know, it's pathetic, it really is. Look at you. What are you scared of? How many times do I have to explain it to you? When you going to let go of this fear? Jesus! Fucking Jews! The thing with the fucking Jews is . . .

Benny *slaps* **Ruben**. *Pause*

Benny   All right? Now, that's enough. (*Pause.*) I don't care what happens any more. Make your phone call, get us killed, do what you want. This is my fault, I agreed to this and I'm not blaming anyone. But I'm not listening to your shit any more. Not any more. Every day there's someone calling me Jew – like that's an insult. I take that because I think – that's nothing. Call me a Jew – that's not an insult to me, Ruben. But to hear you coming out with the same shit – it . . . it makes me sick.

Ruben   Have you being listening to me? It doesn't matter what we were born . . .

Benny   IT MATTERS! WHO THE FUCK DO YOU THINK YOU ARE? You have two uncles, you have two aunts who died . . . who were murdered because it matters. What is it, Ruben? They're not enough for you? You want to help this goy kill a few more of us?

Ruben   Mr Kray is not going to kill us, Benny! You know what he said in there? He said . . . he said he felt I was like his brother and . . .

Benny (*quietly*)   I'm your brother, Ruben.

Ruben   . . . that . . . I know that. I know you're my . . .

Benny   I'm your brother. I'm sorry you don't want me to be your brother. I'm sorry you don't want to be a Jew. I'm sorry for you, really I am. I'm sorry for what Dad did. I'm so sorry. All my life I've felt sorry for that, but this is the thing . . . I didn't do it. I'm not taking the blame. You understand? You can't blame me for what happened. You can't blame the Jews for what happened.

Ruben   What are you talking about? This has got nothing to do with Izzy. I . . . started all this for you! To save your cinema!

Benny   No, you didn't. You did this for you. This is your adventure. I'm the fucking excuse for you to see if you're . . . if you're something special. You want to be someone else, Ruben? I'll help you. You're not my brother. From this day on. You're not my brother. And you know something else? My uncle – my father's brother – he died over there – he was murdered there – because he knew who he was. He knew he was a Jew. He was special. You . . . you're nothing. *Shum davar*. You're not a Jew. You don't have the right to be a Jew. From this day on.

Pause. **Benny** *turns away from and crossing to a chair, sits down.*

Moon   Ruben? I'm sorry. (*To* **Reg**.) I'm sorry Mr Kray. And I know Beck is too. Aren't you Beck?

Beck *sits down.*

Moon   Um . . . Ruben? Can we still have our money? When you make the call?

Ruben   What?

Moon   When you make the call – can we still have our share? Only it's twelve now. (*Pause.*) I mean, if you're going to ring . . .

Ruben   What? (*Pause.*) Yeah. Yeah. The phone call.

He crosses to the phone. Unseen by the others **Benny***'s eye has been caught by something on the newspaper sheet on the floor. He picks it up and reads it.* **Ruben** *picks up the paper with the telephone number on it and dials.*

Ruben   Hello. (*Pause.*) Mr Kray? (*Pause.*) We . . . um . . . we have your brother. (*Pause.*) Yeah. Yeah. He is currently being held hostage in a secret location somewhere in . . . in . . . um . . . England. We can assure you that Mr Kray's life is in . . . (**Benny** *stands and crosses to* **Ruben**, *newspaper in hand.* **Ruben** *sees him coming. His voice falters.*) his life is in grave danger. Yeah. Yeah. Grave danger and unless you send four thousand pounds to . . . um . . . to . . .

Benny *takes the receiver from him. He listens for a moment and then hangs up. Pause.* **Ruben** *stares straight ahead.*

Benny   How long, Ruben?

Moon   Benny? Benny, what the fuck are you doing? He was . . . he was sorting out the money there!

Benny   Just tell me how long you've known.

Moon   He was talking to . . . he was talking to . . .

Benny   He wasn't talking to anyone, Moon. There was no one on the other end.

Moon   I don't . . . Ronnie wasn't there?

Benny   No one was there.

Moon   Like a – a wrong number?

Benny   Yeah. Like a wrong number. Ronnie's in London.

Ruben   Why are you trying to spoil this, Benny? Why?

Moon   Maybe I wrote it down wrong. It might be me. I bet I wrote it down wrong. It'll be me. Let's just . . . Mr Kray? Could you give us the number again? (*Pause.*) Mr Kray? Could you . . . could you . . . Wait a minute. How do you know he's in London?

Benny   Because he's in the fucking newspaper. Nice big photo. Ronnie. This morning. In London.

Moon   He's . . . He's . . . OK. OK. This is . . . we get a number. We go back to what we were going to do. We ring him! We tell him! We've got Reg! That's . . . that hasn't changed. Benny! I'm saying . . . We've still got him!

Benny   We've got nothing.

Moon   We ring him and and and . . .

Benny *crosses to him and holds up the newspaper sheet.*

Benny   It's not him! All right? It's not him. Reg is in the photo too. Both of them. They've been arrested. Last night. Returning from the North.

Moon   But . . . but . . .

Ruben   He's lying. Whatever he . . . he's lying.

Benny   How long have you known, Ruben? You said you saw the papers this morning? How long have you fucking known?

Moon   It's not him?

Benny   He doesn't even look like him, for fuck's sake.

Moon   But, then who the fuck is this?

Benny   I don't know. He's . . . I don't know. He's no one. Funny, isn't it? Ruben said he came here looking for someone to fuck.

Moon   But . . . but he said. He told us . . .

Beck *suddenly kicks out at the table. He kicks the chair over.*

Beck   Lying fucking bastard lying fucking bastard liars!

Pause.

Moon   There isn't going to be any money?

Ruben   Why are you doing this?

Beck   I nearly fucking . . . I almost . . . I could have done it.

Ruben   Why are you trying to take him away from me, Benny? Why are you trying to do it again?

Pause. **Benny** *stares at him.*

Benny   Oh, Ruben.

He steps forward and puts his hands on **Ruben**'s *shoulder.* **Ruben** *begins to cry.* **Benny** *hugs him.*

Kayn aynhoreh, yingaleh.

Pause. **Ruben** *stabs* **Benny** *in the chest. Silence.* **Ruben** *pulls free; looks away.*

Ruben (*generally*)   There. All right? There. Are you . . . All right? There! Now maybe.

Benny *walks away. He sits.*

Moon   What did you do? Did you . . . ? What did he do?

BeckP   Benny?

He crosses to him.

Benny, are you all right? Benny?

Moon   Did he?

Beck   Benny? Benny?

Benny   Yeah?

Beck   Are you all right?

Moon *crosses to them.*

Moon   Fucking hell! Look at . . . He's pissing blood. He's pissing blood! Benny?

Benny   Yeah.

Moon   Do something, Beck! He's . . . look at that! Look at that! Get a doctor, or something! Beck man! (*Pause.*) Beck!

Benny   Yeah.

Moon   Do something, Beck! He's . . . look at that! Look at that! Get a doctor, or something! Beck, man! (*Pause.*) Beck!

Beck   What!? Do what? He's going man! He's . . . he's . . .

Moon   Oh Jesus! Benny? Can you hear me? Benny!

Beck *is leaving.*

Moon   Beck! Beck! We cannot just . . .

Beck *exits.*

Moon   Beck!

He looks at **Benny** *and then runs after* **Beck**. *Pause.* **Ruben** *glances around.*

Ruben   There . . .

Pause.

Reg   First time I killed someone I felt as light as a feather. Like a bird I was. Top of the world.

Ruben   There.

He takes out the gun.

Reg   I was in Soho, with Ronnie. Afterwards. We was walking down the street, and I could barely feel the pavement.

Ruben *puts the gun in his mouth.*

Reg   I swear to God. Light as a feather. Ronnie said to me – how does it feel then? Course he'd done it lots of times.

Ruben *pulls the trigger. A click. He tries again. A click.*

Reg   And I said that . . .I said, 'Top of the World'.

Pause.

It's not real.

Pause. **Ruben** *holds up the gun and looks at it. He laughs.*

Ruben   Ask . . . (*He laughs.*) Ask me how it feels.

Reg   How does it feel?

The light shrinks on **Ruben**.

Ruben   Like nothing. Like I'm not even here. Like even while you're looking at me I'm just gonna . . . disappear.

Fade to black. Music.